AF540875

TEXTBOOK OF MICROBIOLOGY AND BIOTECHNOLOGY

By

Mr. Adarsh K. Mujapara

&

Dr. Kena P. Anshuman

DISCOVERY PUBLISHING HOUSE PVT. LTD.

NEW DELHI-110 002

Published by:
Tilak Wasan
DISCOVERY PUBLISHING HOUSE PVT. LTD.
4383/4B, Ansari Road, Darya Ganj
New Delhi-110 002 (India)
Phone : +91-11-23279245, 43596064-65
Fax : +91-11-23253475
E-mail : discoverypublishinghouse@gmail.com
sales@discoverypublishinggroup.com
web : www.discoverypublishinggroup.com

First Edition: **2012**

Reprinted: **2017**

ISBN: 978-93-5056-123-2

Textbook of Microbiology and Biotechnology

© Authors

All rights reserved. No part of this publication should be reproduced, stored in a retrieval system, or transmitted in any form or by any means: electronic, mechanical, photocopying, recording or otherwise, without the prior written permission of the author and the publisher.

This book has been published in good faith that the material provided by authors is original. Every effort is made to ensure accuracy of material, but the editor, publisher and printer will not be held responsible for any inadvertent error(s). In case of any dispute, all legal matters are to be settled under Delhi jurisdiction only.

Printed at:
Infinity Imaging Systems
Delhi

PREFACE

"Take interest, I implore you, in those sacred dwellings which one designates by the expressive term: laboratories. Demand that they be multiplied, that they be adorned. These are the temples of the future – temples of well-being and of happiness. There it is that humanity grows greater, stronger, better."

Louis Pasteur
(French chemist, founder of microbiology, 1822–1895)

This book is a selection of Microbiology organized in a logical sequence of topics starting with different aspects, progressing through structure, physiology and taxonomy of pathogenic microbes such as Bacteria, Fungi, Viruses, and Parasites. It is indented as an examination guide in medical microbiology for students of microbiology and biotechnology seeking admission in Postgraduate Courses and other competitive examinations. The material of this book is essentially based on recent achievements in the domain of microbiology, and to its credit many standard textbooks and many individual articles were consulted while writing the manuscript.

This modernized revision of the Microbiology Question bank makes the students aware of the wide range of clinical problems due to microbial pathogens disclosed by recent research. Questions dealt within it have been designed in keeping in view the general trends in paper setting for various examining bodies in the USA, UK, Australia, Netherlands, Canada, India and so on, and therefore it can be confidently predicted that similar questions will definitely be asked in the future examinations too.

This book includes short questions from different areas of Microbiology and biotechnology in a simple style so that the students can quickly revise their subject knowledge and remember the key points in the examinations. It can be used in conjunction with any standard text on the subject.

Adarsh Mujapara & Kena Anshuman

CONTENTS

ABBREVIATIONS

µg	Microgram
µl	Micro litre
µm	Micro metre
cm	Centimetre
DNA	Deoxyribonucleic acid
RNA	Ribo nucleic acid
bp	Base-pair
dNTPs	Dinucleotide triphosphate
R.A.	Rheumatoid arthritis
O.A.	Osteo arthritis
S.N.	Sero negative cases of arthritis
R.F.	Rheumatoid factor
ANA	Anti nuclear antibody
PCR	Polymerase chain reaction
SDS	Sodium dodecyl sulphate
UV	Ultra violet rays
O.D.	Optical density
pH	Minus log of concentration of hydrogen ion
HLA gene	Human leukocyte antigen gene
CAD	Coronary Arterial Disease
Anti CCP	Anti cyclic citrullinated peptide antibody
SNP	Single nucleotide polymorphisms
TNF	Tumour necrosis factor
Pts	patients
CNS	Central nervous system
CLL	Chronic lymphoblastic leukaemia
CML	Chronic myelogenous leukaemia
HTLV-1	Human T-cell leukaemia virus—I
PHA	Phytohematoaggutinin

CEN	Centromere
ABL	Abelson leukaemia virus
HCL	Hairy Cell Leukaemia
SCT	Stem cell transplantation
HLA	Human leukocyte antigen
FISH	Fluorescence *in situ* hybridization
Inv	Inversion
DEL	Deletion
Rx/rxn	Reaction

General Microbiology

History

Q. Microbial world was discovered in the year

A. 1673

Q. Credit for the first vaccine for the prevention of human disease is generally given to:

A. Edward Jenner for the prevention of small pox.

Q. Pasteur credited with discovery of

A. Rabies vaccine, pasteurization, immunization Autoclave

Q. Who discover Anthrax vaccine?

A. L. Pasture

Q. The first human disease proved to have a viral etiology was:

A. Yellow fever

Q. Electron microscope was invented by:

A. Ruska

Q. Which is a recent addition to the Koch's postulates?

A. Specific antibodies to the bacteria should be demonstrated

Q Antibodies were first discovered by :

A. Von behring

Q. Scientific chemotherapy of infections was first used by :

A. Domagk

Q. What was the first successful solid medium for colony purification of bacteria?

A. Potato

Q. Louis Pasteur established the modern era of food microbiology in 1857 when he showed that microorganisms cause ______ spoilage.

A. Milk

Q. Approximately when did life on earth arise and what evidence do we have that supports this time frame?

A. Life arose approximately 3.5-3.8 billion years ago. We know this based on fossil evidence of cyanobacterial cells (microfossils) and fossilized bacterial communities called stromatolites.

Q. Life on earth may be divided into two major categories. What are they and what major feature distinguishes between them?

A. Prokaryotic – lacks a nucleus; literally "before a nucleus (primitive)". Eukaryotic – contains a nucleus; literally "true nucleus (well develop)".

Q. What is Cell?

A. Cell is the smallest structural unit of living organisms that is able to grow and reproduce independently.

Q. Briefly explain cell theory.

A. The theory that all living things are comprised of cells and cells are defined by a bounding membrane.

Q. What is the main usefulness to the Microbial Classification? (That is why I should care about taxonomy)

A. The usefulness is the identification of a particular isolate as belonging to a homogeneous group that shares important biological properties.

Q. What is the difference between Phyletic and phonetic classification?

A. Phyletic systematic are based on molecular genetic similarity whereas phenetic classification is based on morphology (phenotypic similarities).

Q. What are some phenotypic similarities that are used when classifying bacteria?

A. Morphology, Staining

Q. Difference between Eukaryote/Prokaryote

A. Eukaryote: sexual reproduction- example: Algae, fungi

Prokaryote: asexual division- example: Bacteria

Q. 'The father of Genetics"
A. G.J. Mendel
Q. The five kingdom concept was proposed by
A. Whittaker
Q. Who is the well known Indian paleobotanist?
A. Birbal Sahni
Q. First plant viruses were discovered in which plant?
A. Tobacco
Q. Who is the founder of binomial nomenclature?
A. Cark Linnaeus
Q. Streptomycin was discovered by
A. waksman
Q. Penicillin was discovered by
A. Alexander Fleming
Q. Who has discovered the cell?
A. Robert Hook
Q. W.M. Stanley got Nobel Prize for
A. Virus
Q. T/F Morgan and Muller showed that chromosomes contain DNA
A. TRUE
Q. Who discovered Polymerase Chain Reaction (PCR)?
A. Kary Mullis

Microscopy

Q. Use of Light Microscope
A. Used in bacteriology Examination of un/stained smears
Q. In short Electron Microscope:
A. Detailed structure of pro/eukaryotic observed
2 Types: TEM/SEM
TEM : Good for minute particles/viruses
SEM : Good for 3-D images of surface of micro.org by use of shadowing technique or freeze-drying specimens
Q. Dark field Illumination:
A. Performed on dark microscope, Creating a darkfield contrasting against the highlighted edge of specimen used of observing spirochetes Ex: *Treponnema pallidum*

Q. Phase-phase microscope

A. Different phases are converted into different intensities so that some structures appear darker than others.

Q. Confocal Microscope

A. Laser light beams, Provide 3-D image from thick fluorescent specimen useful in cell biology

Q. True or False: On our class microscopes, immersion oil should only be used with the 100 X objectives, and not with any other objectives.

A. False

Q. If you are using a compound microscope with a 10X eyepiece and a 40X Objective, the overall magnification of your sample will be:

A. 400X

Q. The resolving power of light microscope is limited by :

A. Wave length of light

Q. The resolving power of an electron microscope is :

A. 0.2nm

Q. What is the magnification of the low power objective lens?

A. 10X (Low Power)

Q. What is the total magnification of the low power, objective lens multiplied by the power of the Ocular Lens?

A. 100X (10X10)

Q. How can an accurate measurement of a cell be established?

A. By using to ocular micrometer and a stage micrometre.

Q. What is the formula for finding the accurate measurement of a cell, using the ocular micrometre and the stage micrometre?"

A. *(# of stage divisions) (10 um)* = one ocular value in µm (calibration factor

(# of ocular divisions)

Lab environment

Q. What is optical density?

A. Optical density = minus logT.

Q. What is end point analysis?

A. Serum sample and reagents are mixed and incubated for a fixed time, to develop the colour optimally. Then, the OD is ascertained and the concentration of the substances is calculated. This is called end point analysis.

Q. What is kinetic method?

A. Serum and reagents are incubated, and readings are taken at 2 and 3 minutes exactly, and from the difference in OD between the two values, the concentration is calculated. Here the optimum colour is not developed, but is quicker and hence is often used in autoanalysers.

Q. What is accuracy?

A. Accuracy is the closeness of a result to the true value.

Q. What is meant by the term precision?

A. Precision refers to the reproducibility of the result. Precision depends on the technique, the reagents, as well as on the technician.

Q. What is meant by specificity?

A. Specificity of a reaction denotes that only one substance will answer that particular test.

Specificity is determined by the method of the analysis.

Q. What are anticoagulants?

A. Anticoagulants prevent the clotting of blood and these are used for the separation of plasma.

Q. What is the difference between serum and plasma?

A. Fibrinogen is absent in serum and fibrinogen is present in plasma.

Q. How do you wash the test tubes, beakers, volumetric flasks, And glass cylinders etc.?

A. Soak the glassware in the detergent solution for few hours and then wash them with the tap water. Afterwards rinse them with the distilled water and keep them in hot air oven for one hour.

Q. Physical agents use for Methods of Sterilization

A. Dry heat (oven: 160^0 C), Moist heat (autoclave: 121° C), Radiation (UV light), Filtration (candles, asbestos pads), Ultrasonic vibrations

Q. Chemical agents use for Methods of Sterilization

A. Alcohol (70% concentration), Phenol, Heavy metal ions, Oxidizing agents, Detergents (soaps)

Q. Why we use 70 per cent alcohol for hand sterilization?

A. Evaporation time is longer than then 100 per cent alcohol penetration power of water is good then the alcohol water is give speedy penetration in bacterial cell wall.

Q. Full form of HEPA filter

A. High efficiency particulate air filter.

Q. General pore size of HEPA filter

A. 0.3 micron

Q. *In Vitro* (outside the body) anti-septic/antibiotic susceptibility testing depends on:

A. Type of medium used, Quantity of organism (inoculum), Incubation period

Q. Which is most occurring pathogen (FUNGI)?

A. *Candida albicans*

Q. What colour is the micro fungi *penicillium*?

A. Green to bluish-gray

Q. Tardigrades are also known by what other name?

A. Water bears

Q. There are three types of protists, one of which is animal-like. What is the term used to describe the animal-like protists?

A. Protozoans

Q. The other two types of protists are plant-like and fungi-like. Although fungi-like protists do not have a term to describe them, what is the term used to characterize plant-like protists?

A. algae

Q. There are four ways in which a protozoan can move:

A. They can either move by using flagella, cilia, spores, or pseudopodia.

Q. What are pseudopodia?

A. Cytoplasm containing extensions

Q. There are four main groups of protozoans:

A. Amoebas, flagellates, ciliates, and sporozoans.

Q. Which disease does plasmodium cause?

A. Malaria

Q. Green algae alternate between living as a haploid organism, which is an organism with only one set of chromosomes, and a diploid organism, which is an organism with two sets of chromosomes. What is the term used to describe the haploid form of an organism?

A. Gametophyte

Q. _______ produce zygospores.

A. Black bread molds/*mucor*

Q. _______ produce motile sexual and asexual spores.

A. Water molds

Q. _______ produce ascospores in an ascus.

A. class:- *Ascomycetes*

Q. _______ produce basidiospores

A. Class:- *Basidomycetes*

Q. Complex algal toxins, most of which are temperature stable, are known to cause peripheral neurological system effects, often in less than ________ after ingestion.

A. one hour

Q. What does the phrase, "Microorganisms are ubiquitous", mean?

A. Microorganisms are everywhere.

Q. Which one of the following is a major green house gas?

A. CO_2

Q. An example for a parasitic algae is

A. Cephaleuros

Q. Atmospheric nitrogen can be fixed by

A. Anabaena

Q. Western Blot test is used in the diagnosis of

A. AIDS

Q. Number of chromosomes in an organism is maintained by the following division.

A. meiosis

Q. Cell wall is chemically made up by

A. Lignin, pectin and cellulose

Q. Pasteurization of milk destroys ?

A. The process destroys pathogenic bacteria

Q. Algin is obtained from which type of algae?

A. brown algae.

Q. 'Pond silk' is the common name of which fungi?

A. Spirogyra

Q. Use of Herbicide

A. To kill the weeds

Q. Streptomycinis produced from

A. Streptomyces griseus

Q. Iodine is obtained from

A. Gelidium

Q. Bacteria generally multiply by which method?

A. Binary fission

Q. Agaar-agar is obtained from

A. Gelidium

Q. Which bacteria produce vinegar in sugar solution?

A. Acetobacter aceti

Q. Direct cell division is otherwise known as

A. Amitosis

Q. Which medicine is used in the treatment of AIDS?

A. Azidothymidine

Q. The organic compounds that contain nitrogen

A. Protein

Q. Lysosomes are known as

A. Suicide bags

Staining

Gram Staining

Q. Name a primary stain and explain what it does?

A. A primary stain is the first reagent used in the process of the Gram Stain. It is Gram's crystal violet and stains all the cells purple. It is a positive stain.

Q. Which stains are used in gram stain?

A. Crystal violet, safranin.

Q. Gram positive and gram negative are separated by what feature?

A. Their cell wall composition.

Q. Which type of bacteria (gram positive or negative) has a complete outer membrane including lippolysaccharide LPS?

A. Gram Negative.

Q. Difference between Gram (+) ve and Gram (-) ve cells:

A. A. Gram (+) ve: - Teichoic acid, Thick, Peptidoglycan, Blue Gram stain

B. Gram (-) ve: - Outer membrane containing LPS, Thin, Peptidoglycan, Red Gram stain, Endotoxin, symptoms (fever, shock)

Q. Which types of bacterial cells can be stained by the simple staining procedure (Using Methylene blue) that you performed in class?

A. Both Gram positive and Gram negative cells

Q. Crystal violet acts as the:

A. Primary stain

Q. The acetone-alcohol is used to:

A. Wash crystal violet out of gram negative cells

Q. in grams staining grams iodine act as:

A. Mordent.

Q. Gram positive cells retain crystal violet dye in the Gram staining procedure because they

A. Have a thicker Peptidoglycan layer than gram-negative cells

Q. What is the role of crystal violet in the performance of a gram stain?

A. Stain

Q. Gram staining technique was developed by:

A. Hans Christian gram 1884

Q. The Gram stain differentiates between bacteria based on the composition of their ________.

A. Cell Wall

Q. What colour do Gram positive and Gram negative bacteria take; respectively?

A. Purple and Pink

Q. Doing a Gram stain from a culture in broth simply requires the use of a few loops of culture. However, if you want to do a stain from colonies on media, what compound must you add a drop of to the microscope slide beforehand?

A. Water (distilled water).

Q. Before you use your reagents to stain the bacteria, you need to heat fix your sample first by waving the slide through the blue flame on a bunsen burner a few times. Why do you do this?

A. So that the bacteria will not be washed off

Q. _______ is the first reagent used in the Gram's stain. You have to wait 30 seconds before tipping it off and washing your slide with water.

A. Crystal Violet

Q. _______ is the second reagent used in the Gram's stain. You have to wait 30 seconds before tipping it off and washing your slide with water.

A. Iodine

Q. What is the charge of a basic stain?

A. Positive

Q. What is the charge of an acidic stain?

A. Negative

Q. What is a Gram Stain?

A. The Gram Stain is the most important differential stain used in Microbiology.

Q. What is the gram nature of Staphylococcus Aureus?

A. Gram +, coccus, in clusters

Q. Name two gram-rods.

A. *Escherichia coli, Serratia marcescens*

Acid fast staining

Q. What is acid fast stain?

A. Some bacteria resist discolouration of acid alcohol after staining by carbol-fuchsin.

Q. Are acid-fast bacteria a gram positive or negative bacteria and why are they called 'Acid-fast'?

A. They are technically gram positive but cell wall is loaded with lipids—thick greasy waxy cell wall. (Hard for substances to get in or out of cell... slow growing).

Q. Acid fastness inability to stain due to: High concentration of Lipids called:

A. Mycolic acids granules (metachromatic granules)

Q. What are the two stains used for the acid-fast stain?

A. Kinyoun carbol fuchsin (primary ZNCF), Aqueous methylene blue (counter-stain) OR malachite green.

Other

Q. What is a negative stain?

A. A negative stain is one which stains the background of a slide. It is acidic.

Q. Name a negative stain.

A. Nigrosen, eosin, or Acid fuchsin

Q. What are the three criteria for endospore?

A. Location, shape, size

Q. What stains are used for an endospore stain?

A. Malachite green, Gram's safranin, ZNCF.

Q. What is a capsule stain?

A. It is a stain which allows the viewing of a capsule on an organism.

Q. How do you spread a slide for a capsule stain?

A. Hold a slide at approximately a 45° angle and 'back it into' the bacteria-albumin mixture. Allow it to spread across the junction of the 2 slides, THEN, push the slide forward across the surface of the slide to make a thin smear.

Q. What is Motility?

A. Movement of a bacteria

Q. How would you observe motility in bacteria?

A. By wet mount or by inoculating a motility medium.

Media

Q. What do you call a solution containing the nutrients for an organism to survive?

A. Culture Medium

Q. What is Agar?

A. An extract of seaweed.

Q. What are the three types of Media commonly used in a Microbiology Lab class?

A. Broth, Semi-solid, Solid

Q. What are the three types of Solid Media commonly used in a Microbiology Lab class?

A. Agar Slant, Agar Deep, Agar Plate

Q. What should you do to organisms in a broth before using them to culture plates?

A. Re-suspend organisms in the broth by gently 'flicking/agitating' the upright tube.

Q. What are you looking for when inoculating a Nutrient gelatin tube?

A. Liquefaction period.

Q. What are the seven different types of growth you might observe on an agar slant?

A. Filiform, Echinulate, Beaded, Spreading, Effuse, Arborescent, Rhizoid

Q. What are Bacteria called that require enrichment with plant and animal extract?

A. Fastidious

Q. How is turbidity measured?

A. The spectrophotometer is used to measure the amount of light transmitted (%t) or absorbed (O.D. = optical density).

Q. What is a Selective Media used for?

A. Selective media are used to suppress the growth of unwanted bacteria and encourage the growth of desired ones. The media 'selects for' a certain group of organisms. It is used for a culture with mixed organisms.

Q. 5 Basic ways to manipulate, grow, examine, and characterize microorganisms

Q. The 5 I's of Microbiology

A. Inoculation, Incubation, Isolation, Inspection, Identification.

Q. Work of MacCokey agar:

A. Selective for gram negative, differ for lactose fermenters (pink) and non-fermenters (pale)

Q. Lactose fermenters

A. 2 scenarios:

(1) Multiple acid waste products (lactic acid, formic acid, acetic acid) from fermentation build up in growth and media surrounding growth and produce a large hot pink coloration—ex. *Escherichia coli*

(2) Single acid waste products (acetic acid) from fermentation builds up in growth and produces hot pink coloration—ex. *Enterobacter aerogenes*

Q. Non-lactose fermenters

A. No fermentation occurring so there is no acid waste, so no pH change, no colour change. Growth occurs and remains transparent.

Q. About EMB Agar:

A. Eosin Methylene Blue Agar, Selective and differential media for gram negative intestinal bacteria(eg: *E.coli*).

Q. What is Blood Agar and what does it differentiate?

A. General isolation media differential for hemolytic action (α, β, and γ heamolysis).

Q. Work of Thioglycollate medium?

A. Decrease gaseous diffusion aerobic, micro aerobic and anaerobic conditions at different depths.

Q. Selinite enrichment broth use for?

A. Enriches for *Salmonella/Shigella.*

Q. Full form SS Agar

A. *Salmonella – Shigella* Agar.

Q. What does it differentiate form S.S. agar?

A. Differentiate for lactose fermenters (pink) and H_2S production (black centre)

Q. Mannitol Salt Agar work

A. Differentiates for *Staphylococcus aureus* (Mannitol farm) —> yellow

Q. Brilliant green agar use for?

A. Selective media for salmonella (—> red/pinkish)

Q. What is PEA agar?

A. Phenyl ethyl Alcohol Agar, Decrease gram negative growth (frees gram +)

Q. Which agar plate is used to grow fungus?

A. Sabauroud Dextrose, Potato Dextrose Agar .

Q. A culture medium like MSA on which only salt-tolerant organisms grow and only Staphylococcus aureus consistently causes the media to change to a yellow colour is called?

A. Selective medium

Q. About Chocolate agar

A. Specifically used for cultivating fastidious bacteria *Neisseria and* streptococci species,. To show presence, we add the Oxidase reagent and look for purplish colouration change.

Q. About Mueller-Hinton-Tellurite

A. Used to cultivate Diphtheroids species of Corynebacterium genus. Bacteria will grow black due to the precipitation of the metal tellurium from within the medium.

Q. About Sabouraud's agar

A. Acidic, specifically used to grow yeasts (slimy growth) and molds (fuzzy growth).

Q. Sodium thioglycollate media

A. Creates an anaerobic environment. Pink layer at top indicates Oxygen is bound to resazurin, a reducing agent.

Q. Function of Mannitol Salt Agar

A. Selective for *Staphylococcus* species, *halotolerant* species, differentiates *Staphylococcus xylosus* (and *Staphylococcus aureus*) and others that ferment mannitol.

Q. Contains of Mannitol Salt Agar

A. Contains 7.5% NaCl, phenol red (pH indicator), and mannitol (substrate). The yellowing of the media is caused by the fermentation of mannitol and the production of acidic wastes, which causes the pH to drop.

Q. Blood agar

A: Differentiates based on hemolytic reactions: α–greenish/grey tint around colonies; β–complete clearing of media around colonies; γ– no change of media around colonies.

Q. Sodium nitrite is responsible for

A. Protecting against botulism, reducing rate of spoilage, maintenance of red colour in meat.

Q. What does TSA stand for?

A. Tryptic(ase) Soy Agar

Q. What is a Rose agar plate used for? What is in it?

A. Rose agar is selective for Gram positive bacteria. It consists of TSA plus 5% sheep's blood which contains C.N.A. plus PEA, which inhibit the growth of Gram negative bacteria.

Q. Rose Bengal Agar used for:

A. Cultivation of mould and inhibit bacterial growth

Q. What would you call an organism that grows throughout a TSA deep?

A. Facultative Anaerobe

Q. What would you call an organism that grows only at the bottom of a TSA deep?

A. Strict Anaerobe

Q. Coagulase Test means?

A. Detect ability to clot plasma

Q. What is oxidation Fermentation test used for?

A. Differentiate gram negative intestinal genera from *Enterobacteriaceae.* Glucose Fermentors: *Enterbacteriaceae, Staphyloccus*

Q. What is the Indole positive colour?

A. Red

Q. About CAMP test

A. Looks for synergistic homology

Q. Describe catalase test

A. Catalase present in bacteria to prevent effects of hydrogen peroxide, ex: (positive) for *E. Coli, pseudomonas,* + *staphylococcus ; (negative) streptococcus.*

Q. DNAse Test (with bacteria)??

A. If bacteria produce DNAse you will see a clear zone.

Q. Describe oxidase test

A. Detects presence of cytochrome oxidase system invovled in aerobic respiration and permits H_2O_2 production.

Q. The effectiveness of many chemical preservatives depends primarily on the food

A. pH

Q. What are the three different types of organisms labelled for the effects of temperature?

A. Psychrophiles, Mesophiles, Thermophiles

Q. What are the optimal temperatures for each: Psychrophiles, Mesophiles, Thermophiles?

A. -5°C - 20°C, 20°C - 45°C, 35°C - 60°C

Q. What are the three different types of pH called?

A. Acidophile, neutrophile, alkalinophile

Q. What are the optimum pH levels for each; Acidophile, neutrophile, alkalinophile

A. pH 0-5.4, pH 5.5-8.4, pH 8.5-11.5

Q. What do TDT and TDP stand for?

A. Thermal Death Time, Thermal Death Point

Q. What is the difference between TDT and TDP?

A. Thermal Death Time is how long it takes an organism to die at a given temperature. Thermal Death Point is the minimum temperature required to kill an organism.

Q. What are the three levels of solute investigated for tonicity?

A. Isotonic, Hypotonic, Hypertonic

Q. What is the term used to describe a cell that has dehydrated?

A. Plasmolysis

Q. What size of wavelength is microbicidal?

A. 300 nm and below

Q. Damage to the bacterial chromosome that results in lethal mutation happens when:

A. DNA absorbs UV light with resultant thymine-thymine dimers formed.

Bacteriology

Q. What is the difference between swabs for viruses and bacteria?

A. Viral swabs contain antibiotics.

Q. Name a well known *Arcanobacterium* and where is it found?

A. Pyogenes—found in normal flora on surface of the skin

Q. What is the general appearance of *Clostridium*?

A. Spindle shaped with flagella.

Q. which anaerobe accounts for 1/3 of bacteria in feces?

A. Bacteroides fragilis.

Q. Obligate aerobes

A. Will have growth concentrated at top of tube only

Q. Microaerophiles

A. Will have growth about ¼-1/2 inch below the top of tube.

Q. Obligate anaerobes

A. Will have growth in the bottom of the tube only.

Q. Aerotolerant anaerobes

A. Will consistent growth throughout the tube.

Q. Facultative anaerobes

A. Will have consistent growth throughout the tube but will also have an extra pad of growth at the top of the tube.

Q. What gives bacteria their shape and provides rigid support:

A. Peptidoglycan layer in cell wall not in human cells therefore, Good target for anti-bacterial drugs, Eg: Penicllin, Cephalosporin inhibiting cell wall synthesis

Q. Type of polysaccharide capsule helpful in serological typing of bacteria and determinant to virulence:

A. Polymerized D-glutamic acid

Q. Capsule in all gram (-)ve except which bacteria?

A. *Anthrax Bacillus*

Q. Function of a capsule .

A. Capsule protects organism from environmental hazards, Serves as antiphagocytic surface, Provides specific adherence

Q. What is Lysosome Enzyme?

A. Present in human tears, mucus, saliva, Can cleave peptidoglycan backbone, Contributes to natural resistance of host to microbial infection

Q. What is Lipopolysaccharide (LPS)?

A. Consist of Lipid-A complex lipids, Endotoxin of gram (-)ve bacteria firmly bound to cell surface, Released only when cell lysed, Target for antibiotics and pyrogenic activity (Fever induction)

Q. Where Purified form of Endotoxin found?

A. Found in outer membrane of gram (-)ve bacteria.

Q. What is Flagella?

A. Mainly in gram (-)ve, Organ of locomotion/motility, Major function: mediate adherence of bacteria to other bacteria/cells

Q. About Pili: Fimbriae:

A. Found mainly in Gram (-)ve, 2 Types: Ordinary pili and Sex pili, Function: Adhesion

Q. Name two Spore forming organisms:

A. *Clostridium, Bacillus* (Both Gram (+)ve) *Clostridium* (anaerobic), *Bacilllus* (aerobic)

Q. Spores are

A. Single internal spore produced under unfavourable conditions such as nutrition depletion)—Resistant to cold, heat, drying, chemical agents possess multiplayer protective coating.

Q. Enterotoxins:

A. Cause food poisoning, Heat stable toxins, Resistant to gut enzymes,

Q. Coagulase

A. Best correlate of pathogenicity, Coverts fibrinogen to fibrin (clot), Allow organism to adhere

Q. Hemolysis

A. Alpha : partial breakdown of RBC

Beta : complete breakdown of RBC

Gamma : no breakdown of RBC

Q. 45-yr-old male with alcohol abuse, periodontal disease, fever/chills, pneumonia with lung consolidation. CXR shows cavity in right lower lung; what type of bacteria involved:

A. Anaerobic bacteria because organism is elsewhere+ causing disease elsewhere (mixed infection)

Q. *Salmonella and Shigella* are differentiated in the lab by:

A. Motility and S.S. agar plate

Q. 6-wk-old infant with 10 days cough/choking; WBC –20% lymphocytes, vomits x2, encapsulated gram (-) ve rods on which media:

A. Triple sugar iron agar or Urease agar

Q. ADP-ribosyl transferase which effects G-regulatory protein causes increase cAMP levels:

A. Pertussis toxin

Q. Paroxysms of cough known as Whooping cough which organism involved:

A. *Bordatella pertussis*

Q. 16-yr-old girl with enlarged lymph node (Right axilla). Blood count – normal; Granulomas with neutrophils + necrotic debris. Which org:

A. *Brucella Henselae* (also responsible for cat scratch disease)

Q. Alcoholic + smoker, dyspnea, headache, muscle pain, fever, chills; which organism involved:

A. *Legionella pneumophillia*

Q. Causes muscle paralysis:

A. Botulinum toxin

Q. The most important for preventive function of the antibody stimulated by Tetanus:

A. To neutralize the toxin of the pathogen

Q. Which organism causes gas gangrene?

A. *Campylobacter Perfringes*

Q. Each is true concerning wound infection caused by perfringens except:

A. Organism grows only in human cell culture

Q. Causes muscle spasms:

A. Tetanus toxin

Q. Causes nyonecrosis:

A. Clostridium alpha-toxin

Q. Virulence tests

A. *In Vitro*—Elk's test (neutralization test/horse serum), *In Vivo*—inoculation and observation

Q. Cause of *Bacillus anthrax*:

A. *Bacillus anthrax* Causes Woolsorters disease

Q. Polyarthritis in knees with cough. Sphirochete shows lyme disease which organism involved:

A. *Borrelia bergdorferi*

Q. Global eradication of lyme disease is unlikely beacause:

A. Can be maintained by tick vector

Q. 19 yr-old patient .with weakness, malaise, dry cough. 100oF; bronchial lavage are slow growing. Org:

A. *Mycoplasma pneumoniae*

Q. Sexually active female experiences lower abdominal-pain, no rash on labia; Smear shows scanty neutrophils. What lab results show?

A. Inclusion bodies due to *Chlamydia*

Q. Patient collapses loss of consciousness, severe lower ab-pain, nausea, shock, ectopic pregnancy. Which organism:

A. *Chlamydia*

Q. 4-yr-old infant with chlamydia trachomonis. Blindness in this patient caused by:

A. Scarring of cornea

Q. Maculopapular rash, shock + renal failure 3 days after returning from camping trip in east USA. Which org responsible for symptoms:

A. *Rickettsia ricketsii* (aka: Rocky mountain spotted fever) due to ticks

Q. Bacteria reproduce using ______________________________. This means that when they reach a maximum size, they split in two.

A. binary fission

Q. Fungi can spread two ways. In both sexual and asexual reproduction they make small light round structures called ________________.

A. spores

Q. What does the Lipase enzyme do?

A. Breaks down lipid/fat/oil molecules

Q. What does the Protease enzyme do?

A. Breaks down protein molecules

Q. How does Lipase help to make the laundry powder clean clothes?

A. Helps any fat/oil/lipid molecules in the dirt/stain to dissolve in the washing water.

Q. How does Lipase help to make the laundry powder clean clothes?

A. Helps any protein molecules in the dirt/stain to dissolve in the washing water.

Q. Which bacteria are associated with cat bites?

A. *Pasteurella multocida* (*Pasteurella multocida* is found in the feline oral cavity and is the most common cause of infection after a cat bite.)

Q. Which of the following is considered a potential agent of bioterrorism?

A. *Franciscella tularensis* (*Franciscella tularensis* is the causative agent of tularemia or rabbit fever. Hunters are at risk for contracting the disease due to contact with animal hides. It can be contracted by inhaling the bacteria which makes it an effective agent of bioterrorism.)

Q. The genus Mycoplasma is resistant to the effects of ____________.

A. Penicillin

Q. Which type of plasmid, when taken up by a bacteria, confers the ability to create a sex pilus?

A. F-plasmid

Q. Which is the most important structure related to microbial attachment to cells?

A. Glycocalix

Q. Endotoxins are secreted from?

A. Endotoxins are secreted from cells (inside).

Q. The Ixodes tick is a transmission factor for which organisms?

A. *Babesia*

Q. Chagas' disease is commonly treated with Nifurtimox and is linked to the ____ microorganism.

A. *Trypanosoma cruzi*

Q. A major advance in the detection of foodborne pathogens is the use of standardized pathogen DNA patterns, or "foodborne pathogen ________".

A. fingerprinting.

Q. The main reservoir of Staphylococcus aureus is

A. human nasal cavity.

Q. Roughly 3% of the known bacteria cause disease and are referred to as ___ __________.

A. Pathogens

Q. Some bacteria only cause disease if the opportunity arises and are referred to as ___ _______.

A. opportunistic pathogens

Q. Bacteria are traditionally divided into two major categories. What are they and what are the differences that distinguish the two categories?

A. Bacteria have been divided into Gram positive and Gram negative. Gram positive bacteria have a thicker cell wall (20-80nm) than Gram negative bacteria (2-7 nm). Gram negative bacteria also have an outer membrane surrounds a thin underlying layer of peptidoglycan.

Q. What is the name of the flagellar arrangement in which a flagellum is found at each end the bacterium?

A. Amphitrichous

Q. Describe function of a cell membrane.

A. The function of a CM is to keep out charged and large molecules (macromolecules).

Q. Name the major chemical elements from which life is composed. Write out the full names please.

A. Carbon, Hydrogen, Oxygen, Nitrogen, Phosphorus and Sulfur

Q. Acetic acid is produced by

A. Gluconobacter and Acetobacter

Q. Most important surface active disinfectant

A. cationic compound, acid anionic surface-active sanitizer

Q. Heat liable instruments for use in surgical procedures can be best sterilized by:

A. Ethylene oxide gas

Q. Organ of adhesion of bacteria

A. Fimbriae

Q. The best skin disinfectant is

A. Betadine

Q. Most of the drug resistance occurs due to

A. Conjugation

Q. Cachetin is produced by

A. Macrophages

Q. Interferon is .... In nature

A. Protein

Q. In the hemolysis test on a blood agar plate, an incomplete hemolysis will show streaks of what colour?

A. Green

Q. What is the primary virulence factor for E. coli?

A. Toxin inhibits protein synthesis

Q. What is the primary virulence factor for N. gonorrhea?

A. Pili/Fimbriae

Q. What is the primary virulence factor for H. influenza?

A. Capsule

Q. The cross-linked bonds are between a terminal D-____ from one chain and a diamino amino acid from the other chain. A pentaglycine bridge (gly5) expands the cross-link in Staphylococcus aureus.

A. Alanine

Q. In the first phase of peptidoglycan synthesis, glucosamine is enzymatically converted to N-acetylmuramic acid (MurNAc), then energetically activated to form what pentapeptide precursor?

A. UDP-MurNAc-pentapeptide

Q. In the third phase of peptidoglycan synthesis, where is the disaccharide:peptide precursor moved to?

A. Outside of the cell

Q. What bacterial cell component is affected by cephalosporin, penicillin, and other ?- lactam antibiotics?

A. Transpeptidases (PBPs)

Q. What is the initial phase of bacterial growth (on the bacterial growth curve) called?

A. Lag phase

Q. *Clostridium perfringens* cannot grow with oxygen present and thus is a(n) ____ while Mycobacterium tuberculosis requires oxygen and thus is a(n) ____.

A. Obligate anaerobe; Obligate aerobe

Q. By what mechanism do pathogenicity (virulence) islands coordinate the expression of a system of virulence factors?

A. Transposons

Q. What is the normal process used by the cell for the uptake of receptor-bound molecules such as hormones, low-density lipoproteins, and transferrin?

A. Endocytosis

Q. Which bacterial virulence mechanism does superantigen fall into?

A. Toxins

Q. Which bacterial virulence mechanism does capsid fall into?

A. Immune response inhibitor

Q. botulinum toxin produced by :

A. *Cl. botulinum*

Q. tetanus toxin produced by:

A. *Cl. tetani*

Q. What is the gene location for the botulinum toxin?

A. Phage

Q. What is the gene location for the tetanus toxin?

A. Plasmid

Q. What is the biological effect of the botulinum toxin?

A. Decrease in peripheral, presynaptic acetylcholine release, flaccid paralysis

Q. What is the biological effect of the tetanus toxin?

A. Decrease in neurotransmitter release from inhibitory neurons, spastic paralysis

Q. What is the biological effect of the cholera toxin?

A. Activation of adenylate cyclase, increase in cAMP level, secretory diarrhoea

Bacillus

Q. Bacillus are ____ spore formers and Clostridium are ____ spore formers.

A. Aerobic and facultative anaerobic; Anaerobic

Q. In non-industrial countries, what is the most likely place to find B. anthracis?

A. Skin/fur of herbivores

Q. A young man enters the Emergency Room dehydrated, afebrile, and complaining of nausea and vomiting. Since he began vomiting one hour ago, he has been 'hugging the toilet' nearly every ten minutes. He remembers eating a dish with fried rice at an Asian restaurant several hours ago. Which organism is most likely the cause?

A. *B. cereus*

Q. Name a well known Bacillus bacterium

A. *Bacillus anthraces*

Q. Can Bacillus bacteria persist in the environment for a longtime? (Why?)

A. Yes. Bacillus are endospore (baby bacteria packaged in thick cell wall—not active and metabolically dormant) forming bacteria—and they can survive in the air.

Q. What are general points to remember for Bacillis bacteria?

A. Endospores

Q. Capsule in all gram (-)ve except which bacteria?

A. *Anthrax Bacillus*

Q. A bacterium (singular) with a rod shape is referred to as a_ ______.

A. Bacillus.

Chlamydia

Q. The Chlamydiaceae life cycle has elemental bodies (EBs) that are ____ and reticulate bodies (RBs) that are ____.

A. Metabolically inactive and infection; Metabolically active and non-infectious

Q. In the life cycle of Chlamydiaceae, ____ bind to cell receptors triggering endocytosis. ____ inhibit lysosome fusion and form ____, which replicate by binary fission and form ____ that cause the cell to lyse.

A. EBs; EBs; RBs; EBs;

Q. *C. trachomatis* would iodine stain ____ and Giemsa stain ____.

A. Positive; Positive

Campylobacter and Helicobacter

Q. Which Test can help differentiate *Campylobacter jejuni* from *Helicobacter pylori* in the laboratory?

A. Urease reaction

Q. A man with fever, muscle pains, and headache feels no need to go to the doctor until about 1 day later, when he develops bloody diarrhoea and abdominal pain as well. The abdominal pain is so severe that his physician fears appendicitis until learning that the man may have had unpasteurized milk in the past week. A definitive diagnosis is made by growth on stool cultures at 42°C, microaerophilic conditions. Which organism is the most likely cause?

A. *C. jejuni*

Q. What disease may be confused with *C. jejuni* because Campylobacter is difficult to detect?

A. Crohn disease

Q. Which organism produces disease resembling Salmonellosis:

A. *Campylobacter jejuni*

Enterococcus

Q. What are the disease patterns of Enterococcus bacteria?

A. Lower UTI Diarrhoea

Q. T/F Enterococcus can live for a long time in the outside environment?

A. True

Q. Abiotrophia and Granulicatella, formerly called nutritionally deficient streptococci, are problematic because they will initially grow in blood culture broths or in mixed cultures but do not grow when subculture onto sheep blood agar media, unless the media is supplemented with pyridoxal, a natural form of what vitamin?

A. Vitamin B6

Enterobacteriaceae

Q. What is the most prevalent Enterobacteriaceae found in gastrointestinal tract infections?

A. *Salmonella or E. coli*

Q. What is the most prevalent Enterobacteriaceae found in urinary tract infections?

A. *Escherichia*

Q. Which of the following is an important cause of hemorrhagic colitis (HC) and hemolytic uremic syndrome (HUS) in the United States?

A. *Enterohemorrhagic E. coli (EHEC)*

Q. Proper cooking of beef products can help reduce the risk of what kind of infections?

A. *Enterohemorrhagic E. coli (EHEC)*

Q. What virulence factor of E. coli is associated with adhesion in the urinary and gastrointestinal tracts and also binds to a blood group antigen?

A. P. pilus AND G. pilus

Q. Bubonic plagues *(Y. pestis)* is characterized by ____ and pneumonic plague *(Y. pestis)* is characterized by ____.

A. 7-day incubation period(death)

A. 3-day incubation period(die)

Q. Two main categories under Gram negative bacteria?

A. *Enterobacteriaceae*

Pasteurellaceae

Q. Name the four sub-categories under Enterobacteriaceae.

A. *Yersinia, Escherichia, Salmonella, Shigella*

Q. Name two categories under Pasteurellaceae.

A. *Haemophilius, Histophilus.*

Q. Name three characteristics of Pasteurella?

A. Cocco-bacillus shape, Positive oxides reaction, Part of normal flora Francisella.

Q. Organism commonly characterized by its O, K, H antigen + ability to ferment lactose:

A. *E.Col i, salmonella*

Q. In the intestinal tract the organism that is lactose fermenting is:

A. *E.coli*

Q. Exotoxin that function as a neurotoxin and enterotoxin

A. *Shigella dysentriae*

Q. Salmonella food poisoning:

A. *S. Typhimurium*

Q. Early in course of Typhoid fever, Salmonella typhi is isolated from:

A. Blood

Q. Which organism is the most common causative agent of urinary tract infections?

A. *Escherichia coli*

Q. *E. coli O157:H7* is thought to have acquired enterohemorrhagic genes from:

A. *Shigella*

Q. A child presents with vomiting and bloody stools. A bacterial culture yields Gramnegative rods that are H_2S negative. Which of the following is most likely?

A. *Shigella*

Haemophilus and Related Bacteria

Q. What are the growth factor requirements for Haemophilus on chocolate agar?

A. Heme and NAD (X and V factors)

Q. How would a person typically acquire a *P. multocida* infection?

A. Cat bite/dog bite

Bordetella, Francisella and Brucella

Q. In *B. pertussis* infection, where is the number of organisms the highest?

A. Respiratory tract

Q. An infant born in a rural area is brought to the ER with severe bouts of coughing throughout the day. During the visit, the baby appears cyanotic and suffers an attack of many coughs on a single expiration followed by a deep inspiration. The cough produces copious greenish phlegm. Further history reveals that the infant has not been vaccinated. The physician fears that erythromycin therapy will not be helpful at this stage of the illness. Which organism is the most likely cause?

A. *B. pertussis*

Q. The ____ version of the pertussis vaccine is associated with unacceptable levels of complications. The ____ version of the vaccine contains inactivated bacteria and the ____ version of the vaccine contains the pertussis toxin and one (or more) bacterial components, which mediate immune response in the host.

A. Whole cell; Whole cell; Acellular

Q. Brucella and Francisella are examples of what kind of disease, where they can be transmitted from animal to human?

A. Zoonosis

Q. What is the primary virulence factor of the intracellular parasite *F. tularensis*?

A. Capsule

Q. Which media use to grow *F. tularensis?*

A. Francis blood dextrose cystine agar

Q. What growth factors are required for *F. tularensis*?

A. Cysteine

Q. 4-yr-old with respiratory distress with 103.8oF fever; drools, difficulty swallowing, stridor. CXR shows epiglottis swelling. Infant has never had a vaccine:

A. *H. Influenzae*

Q. A sexually active male presents with a painful sore (ulcer on his penis) and inguinal lymphadenopathy. Culture reveals Gram-negative coccobacilli that grow on chocolate agar but not blood agar. Which bacteria is the most likely?

A. *Hemophilus ducreyi*

Q. A 1-year-old infant presents with a fever after her parents noticed she was unusually drowsy. The physician notices neck rigidity and occasional seizures. Bacterial culture reveals Gram-negative coccobacilli that grow on chocolate agar and blood agar.

A. *H. influenza*

Listeria

Q. A mother brings her 2-month-old infant to the hospital because he exhibits fever, convulsions, irritability, and poor eating. The paediatrician-in-training notes a widespread rash and a stiff neck on physical exam. She orders a spinal tap, which reveals low glucose, increased PMNs, increased proteins, and Gram-positive rode with 'tumbling' motility in cultures. Upon further questioning, the paediatrician discovers that the mother does not breast feed and feeds her baby fresh cow milk. Which organismis the most likely cause?

A. *L. monocytogenes*

Q. 28 yr-old preg. Women with fever, headache, myalgia, pain and spontaneous abortion:

A. *Listeria monocystogenes*

Q. Neonate with widespread granulomas in uterus:

A. *Listeria monocystogenes* commonly acquired from uterus

Mycoplasma and Ureaplasma

Q. *Mycoplasma pneumoniae* is a common cause of atypical pneumonia (walking pneumonia) and chest x-ray often looks worse than symptoms suggest. Which groups of people is the most commonly affected?

A. School-age children, young adult

Q. Which tests is the most useful currently as an initial laboratory test, has about 65% sensitivity, and has specificity that cross-reacts to other organisms (e.g., Epstein-Barr virus, cytomegalovirus, adenovirus)?

A. Cold hemagglutination

Q. Sterols are present in cytoplasmic membrane of

A. mycoplasma, fungi, plant etc

Mycobacterium

Q. What are the two groups of Acid-fast Bacteria important in Vet Med?

A. *Mycobacterium and Nocardia*

Q. What are the main disease patterns of Mycobacterium?

A. Tuberculosis, granulomatous, enteritis.

Q. What is the treatment and control of Mycobacterium?

A. Chemotherapy for tuberculosis (DOTS).

Q. AIDS patient with chronic cough, has been running low grade fever. CXR is unremarkable. Sputum demonstrates acid-fast organisms. CD4 + T-cells 500/mL. Which causative agent:

A. *M. Avium* Complex

Q. Disfiguring lesions with loss of sensation to touch. Scrapings from skin lesions show which org:

A. *M. Leprae*

Neisseriae

Q. Neisseria are oxidase positive bacteria. What media is used for isolation of Neisseria?

A. Chocolate agar, Thayer-Martin (TM)

Q. Neisseria grows at 35-37 degrees Celsius in a humid atmosphere, with Neisseria gonorrhoea requiring what additional supplement that Neisseria meningitidis does not need?

A. Carbon dioxide

Q. Pili in Neisseria allow for attachment of the bacteria to what kind of cells?

A. Non-ciliated epithelial cells

Q. Phase variation along with antigenic variation account for the ineffectiveness in treating Neisseria infections. Which of the following virulence factors has a variable region at the carboxyl terminus (immunodominant portion of the molecule) leading to antigenic variation?

A. Pilin (protein)

Q. What is the importance of the capsule in the pathogenesis of *Neisseria meningitides* infections?

A. Prevents phagocytosis by the host

Q. Which doesn't influence virulence of *N. gonorrhoea:*

A. Genus specific protein

Q. Neisseria gives oxidase positive or negative:

A. Oxidase (+)ve

Q. Effective vaccines presently in use against meningococceal disease contains which as primary immunogenic agent:

A. Capsular polysaccharide

Q. *Neisseria meningitis*:

A. Differs from other species of neisseria by family of various sugars, oxidase (+)ve, grows in 5-10% CO2, prosses endotoxin

Q. *N. gonorrhoea*:

A. Has pilli if pathogenic, produces penicillin, is oxidase (+)ve, grows best under 10% CO2, may cause blindness in newborns + stertility in women

Q. Frequent bacteria responsible for pharyngitis:

A. *Neisseria meningitis*

Q. Organism most likely to cause conjunctivitis/eye infection in new born if appropriate preventative measures are not taken:

A. *N. gonorrhoea*

Q. Bacteria are cultured and found to be Gram-negative diplococci that grow on chocolate agar and blood agar. Which is the most likely bacteria?

A. Neisseria

Pseudomonas

Q. T/F :- *P. aeruginosa* is inherently resistant to many antibiotics and can mutate (porin proteins) to even more resistant strains during therapy.

A. True

Q. The *P. aeruginosa* virulence factor ____ is a heat-labile hemolysin and the virulence factor ____ is a heat-stable hemolysin.

A. Phospholipase C; Rhamnolipid

Q. In beta hemolysis, a green pigmentation grows in red blood agar. This is due to the ____ pyocyanin and the ____ fluorescein.

A. Blueish green; greenish Yellow

Q. Which patient populations having at high risk for *Burkholderia cepacia* infections of the respiratory tract?

A. Cystic fibrosis patients

Q. Organism most common bacterial pathogen to complilcate (+)ve management of patients with cystic fibrosis:

A. *P. aeruginosa*

Staphylococcus

Q. What does Staphylococcus look like in general?

A. Spherical (coccus) clumps (staphy)

Q. What would a positive coagulase test look for Staphylococcus?

A. They would coagulate at the bottom of the tube Name some Staphylococcus species important in vet medicine *S. aureus, S. hyicus*

Q. What is the major mode of transmission for Staphylococcus?

A. Enter wounds, faces, navel of newborns

Q. What is the most common reservoir site of S. aureus?

A. Skin and mucous membranes

Q. A patient undergoes a procedure to implant a cardiac pacemaker and prosthetic heart valve. One month later, the patient returns with a high fever. Infection is found in the pacemaker pocket, along the pathway of the electrical lead, and near the prosthetic valve. Which bacteria is the most likely cause?

A. *Staphylococcus epidermidis*

Q. *Pneumococci* can be typed by:

A. Swelling of the capsule in the presence of type specific antiserum

Q. The coagulase test, in which the bacteria causes plasma to clot is used to distinguish

A. *Staphylococcus aureus from Staphylococcus Epidermis*

Q. Each of the following concerning *Staphylococcus aureus* is correct except:

A. Treatment should include Beta-Lactamase resistant Penicillin

Q. Which Staphylococcus is part of normal floral of human skin:

A. *Staphylococcus albus*

Q. The principle toxin of Streptococcus Association with virulence is:

A. Streptokinase

Q. Acute glomerulonephritis is associated with:

A. *Streptococcus Pyogenes*

Q. Which organism causes subacute bacterial endocarditis:

A. Alpha-hemolytic streptococcus (*Streptococcus viridans*)

Q. Pneumococci differentiated from *Streptococcus Viridans* is by:

A. Bile solubility

Q. Sub acute bacterial endocarditis caused by a member of viridian of Streptococcus which one is the source of the organism in the infection:

A. Oropharynx

Q. A culture of a skin lesion from a patient with pyoderma (impetigo) shows numerous colonies surrounded by zone of beta-hemolysis on blood agar. A gram stain smear shows gram (+)ve cocci. If you catalase test (-)ve, which of the following organism is to be isolated:

A. *Streptococcus Pyogenes*

Q. What is the most common infection due to Beta-hemolytic streptococcus?

A. Streptococcus Sore throat

Vibrios

Q. Aside from the presence of polar flagella, which of the following laboratory tests can differentiate Vibrionaceae from Enterobacteriaceae?

A. Oxidase reaction

Q. *V. cholerae* O1 and 0139 produce cholera toxin and are associated with epidemics of cholera. The O1 serogroup is divided into ____ (Inaba, Ogawa and Hikojima) and ____(classical and El Tor).

A. Serotypes; Biotypes

Q. In epidemiology, this term refers to an infection in a population where that infection is maintained in the population without the need for external inputs (e.g. *V. cholerae* and chickenpox). Each person who becomes infected with the disease must pass it on to exactly one other person, on average.

A. Endemic

Q. *Vibrio cholera* needs which pH?

A. Marked tolerance for alkaline pH grows at high Ph 8.5-9.5

Miscellaneous Gram-Negative Bacilli

Q. Which Disease is most likely caused by Legionella?

A. legionellosis.

Q. What kind of media is most commonly used to grow Legionella?

A. Buffered charcoal yeast extract agar (BCYE)

Q. What growth factors are required for Legionella?

A. Cysteine and iron

Q. Which laboratory tests used for Legionella detection?

A. Uses indirect fluorescent antibody (IFA)

Q. Nucleic acid amplification assay

A. DNA probe test

Anaerobic, Spore Forming, Gram-positive Rods

Q. A teenage girl enters the emergency room suffering painful muscle spasms. Throughout her examination, she sustains a facial sneer, a stiff arched back, and clamped palms. Her father is anxious about the fact that she has also experienced difficulty eating, probably due to a stiff jaw. The father affirms that her daughter is usually quite active and boasts how, a week ago, she continued a soccer game even after falling on a nail in the field. Which organism is the most likely cause?

A. *Clostridium difficile*

Q. A woman straggles into the emergency room with a marked paralysis of her upper body. She describes the paralysis as a weakness that began in her neck and spread to her arms. She also complains of blurred double vision and requests water to soothe her dry throat. Though she has no fever, she appears quite dizzy and her eyelids are drooping. The day before, she returned from a camping trip where she insists she maintained good hygiene, limiting her diet to canned food only. Which organism is the most likely cause?

A. *Clostridium botulinum*

Q. An old woman comes to the doctor with a fever and loose bowels. Her diarrhoea occurs in tremendous volumes, she complains, though she doesn't remember seeing blood. She has an unremarkable recent past medical history, except for an infection a few weeks earlier that was treated with clindamycin. Sigmoidoscopy of her colon reveals yellow-white plaques which the doctor predicted after analyzing her stools for toxins and colitis. Which organism is the most likely cause?

A. *Clostridium difficile*

Q. A man enters the emergency room claiming to have been stabbed two days earlier. Muscles in his arm hurt, and on palpation small air bubbles are felt below the skin. The wound area exudes a blackish, ill-smelling fluid that generates a crackling sound when touched. The patient has a fever, a low blood pressure, marked tachycardia, and urinated very little since his injury. The doctor decides to amputate the arm, as well as monitor the patient for shock and renal failure. Which of the following is the most likely cause?

A. *Clostridium perfingens*

Anaerobic, Non-Spore Forming, Gram-positive Rods

Q. What is the best description of the shape of Actinomyces?

A. Filamentous

Q. Actinomyces grow ____ in culture and are facultatively anaerobic or strictly ____.

A. Slowly; Anaerobic

Q. Comparing the two, Acinomyces ____ sulfur granules and Nocardia is ____.

A. Form; Acid-fast

Anaerobic Gram-Negative Bacilli

Q. What growth media is used to help differentiate *Bacteroides fragilis*?

A. Bile Esculin agar (BEA)

Q. Bacteroides are the only Gram-negative bacteria without typical:

A. Endotoxin, lipopolysaccharide

Treponema, Borrelia and Leptospira

Q. What stage of syphilis is characterized by disseminating rash, alopecia, lymphadenopathy, and flulike symptoms.

A. Secondary

Q. What is characteristic of primary syphilis?

A. Painless chancre

CHAPTER 5

Biochemistry

Q. What is a sugar?

A. Sugar is a white crystalline substance, soluble in water and sweet in taste. Sugars are classified into two types: (*a*) reducing sugars. (*b*) non-reducing sugars.

Q. What is a reducing sugar? Give examples.

A. Reducing sugar reduces cupric ions in the benedict's and fehling's solutions to cuprous ions and it answers these tests. Examples reducing monosaccharide. Aldohexose: glucose, keto hexose: fructose reducing disaccharides: lactose (milk sugar), maltose (malt sugar, obtained by the hydrolysis of starch) reducing sugars contain sugar groups in their structure.

Q. What is a non-reducing sugar?

A. Non – reducing sugars do not have free sugar group in their structure and they fail to answer benedicts' and fehling's tests. Example sucrose (table sugar)

Q. What are osazones?

A. Reducing sugars react with pheynylhydrazine hydrochloride at 100°c for 30 minutes an Form osazones. Reducing sugars can be identified by seeing the shape of osazones under microscope.

Q. Why glucose, fructose and mannose form same shape of osazones (needle shape)?

A. The spatial configuration of atoms and groups in lower (four) carbons is same in them.

Q. What are proteins?

A. Proteins are polymers of amino acids. There are 20 different amino acids which are present in proteins. These amino acids are joined by peptide linkages.

Q. What are colour reactions of a protein? Give examples.

A. Certain specific reactions give particular colour due to presence of amino acids in their Structures. These are called colour reactions. Example:- ninhydrin reaction blue colour due to presence of alpha-amino acid radical. It is also a general test for the identification of a protein.

Q. Classify the proteins and give examples.

A. Simple proteins example: albumin (egg white), Conjugated proteins example: casein (phosphoprotein present in milk), Derived proteins example: peptones formed by the hydrolysis of a native protein.

Q. What are proteins of high biological value?

A. Proteins of high biological value contain all the essential amino acids in optimum concentration.

Q. What are proteins of low biological value?

A. Proteins of low biological value lack one or two essential amino acids.

Q. What are the properties of proteins at its isoelectric pH?

A. The proteins carry equal number of positive and negative charges, so that it is electrically Neutral, the conductivity and osmotic pressure of a protein solution is at minimum, the solubility is at minimum.

Q. What are the abnormal substances which are likely to be excreted in various diseases?

A. Glucose, ketone bodies, protein (albumin), bile pigments (bilirubin),bile salts.

Q. What is glycosuria (glucosuria)? What are the causes of this Condition?

A. Excretion of glucose in urine is called glycosuria. The causes: diabetes mellitus.

Q. What are the causes of ketonuria?

A. Severe untreated diabetes mellitus, starvation (prolonged fasting).

Q. What are the causes of haematuria?

A. Renal calculus (renal colic), acute glomerulonephritis.

Q. What are the causes of excretion of bilirubin and bile salts?

A. Viral hepatitis, Extra hepatic—gallstones, carcinoma of head of pancreas.

Q. What are the N.P.N. Substances?

A. The non-protein nitrogen (npn) containing substances are :

(*a*) urea (*b*) uric acid (*c*) creatinine

Q. What is normal blood urea level and name the clinical disorders in which it is raised?

A. Normal value : 20 – 40 mg/dl

Pre-renal - dehydration (diarrhoea and vomiting).

Post-renal - renal calculus and enlarged prostrate.

Q. Urea clearance is lowered in which condition?

A. Kidney failure.

Q. What is the maximum urea clearance value?

A. 75 ml/minute.

Q. What is the standard urea clearance value?

A. 54 ml/minute.

Q. When do you call it standard urea clearance?

A. When the volume of urine formed is less than 2 ml per minute.

Q. What is the clinical significance of increased urea level in blood ?

A. Urea level is increased in renal failure.

Q. How failure of concentrating capacity of urine is measured ?

A. Concentration test (Water deprivation test).

Q. What are the usual tests to assess tubular function?

A. Measurement of specific gravity, concentration test, dilution test, acidification test.

Q. What is normal uric acid level and name the clinical disorders in which it is raised?

A. Normal value : Male : 88-135μmol/lit.

Female:- 62-115 μmol/lit. Gout and renal failure.

Q. What is normal creatinine level and name the clinical disorders in which it is raised?

A. Normal value : 0.6 – 1.2 mg/dl. Renal insufficiency and renal failure.

Q. What is the normal value for PAH clearance ?

A. About 700 ml/min.

Q. What is creatinine coefficient?

A. It is the urinary creatinine expressed in mg/kg body weight.

Q. What is the significance of creatinine coefficient?

A. The value is elevated in muscular dystrophy.

Q. What is the normal value of creatinine coefficient?

A. Normal range is 20-28 mg/kg for males and 15-21 mg/kg for females.

Q. What are the parts of photoelectric colorimeter?

A. The following are the parts of photoelectric colorimeter: A source of light, Monochromator, Slit, Cuvette, Photocells

Q. What is beers law and lambert law?

A. Beer's law states that when monochromatic light passes through a colored solution the Amount of light transmitted decreases with the increase in concentration of the coloured Substance *i.e.* The absorbance or optical density increases with the concentration of the Substance.

Lambert's law states that when monochromatic light passes through a coloured solution the Amount of light transmitted decreases with increase in optical path.

Q. What do you record with the colourimeter?

A. The absorbance or optical density of the coloured solution.

Q. Why sodium fluoride is used as a preservative of blood for glucose estimation?

A. To prevent glycolysis and to prevent loss of sugar.

Q. What is normal fasting plasma or serum glucose level?

A. >140 mg/dl.

Q. What is the latest criteria applied for the diagnosis of Diabetes mellitus?

A. When fasting serum glucose is greater than 125 mg/dl and when 2 hours post prandial Serum glucose is 200 mg/dl or more than 200 mg/dl, the patient is diagnosed as diabetes Mellitus.

Q. What is impaired glucose tolerance?

A. When the fasting serum glucose is between 111 mg/dl to 125 mg/dl, it is called impaired glucose tolerance.

Q. What are the different methods of blood sugar Estimation?

A. 1. God–pod (glucose oxidase-peroxidase method),2. Orthotoluidine method.

Q. What are the different methods of blood urea estimation?

A. 1. Berthelot reaction., 2. Dam (diacetylmonoxime) method.

Q. Name the method of estimation of urine creatinine and what is the principle of it?

A. ALKALINE PICRIC METHOD : Creatinine in urine is determined by its reaction with picric acid in an alkaline medium to Form the orange red coloured tautomer of creatinine picrate (jaffe's reaction). Since creatinine Content of urine is high, it is suitably diluted. The intensity of orange colour is read using a Green filter (520 nm).

Q. What is the normal excretion of creatinine per day?

A. 1–2 g/day.

Q. Name the methods for protein estimation :

A. 1.Biuret method 2. Folin and Lowry's method 3.Bradfords method

Q. What is the principle of serum total protein estimation?

A. The peptide bonds of protein react with cupric ions in alkaline solution to form blue-violet Colour complex. The colour formed is proportional to the protein concentration and is measured At 546 nm (520–560 nm).

Q. What is the normal value of serum total proteins?

A. Normal value of total protein – 6.0 – 8.0 g/dl

Normal value of total albumin – 3.2 – 4.5 g/dl

Normal value of total globulin – 2.5 – 3.5 g/dl

A/G Ratio : 1.2 :1 – 2:1

Q. What are the normal values of biochemical substances Present in C.S.F. And give their clinical interpretation?

A. (*a*) Reducing sugar – 40 – 70 mg/dl decrease: meningitis.

(*b*) Proteins – 10 – 40 mg/dl increase: in meningitis and obstruction to flow of c.s.f.

(*c*) Chlorides – 116 to 122 m.mol/dl decrease: meningitis.

Q. What are the important tests included in L.F.T.? Give their Normal values.

A. Serum bilirubin (sb) – 0.2 – 1.0 mg/dl, serum ast. – 8–20 u/l. serum alt – 10–40 u/l, serum alp – 40–125 u/l, direct billirubin: 0.00 -0.2 mg/100ml

Q. What are the substances included in lipid profile and give their normal values?

A. 1. Serum cholesterol 150 – 180 mg/dl desirable borderline upto 200 mg/dl

2. Hdl-cholesterol 40 – 60 mg/dl desirable lower side of borderline 35–39 mg/dl

3. Ldl-cholesterol below 100 mg/dl desirable borderline upto 130 mg/dl

4. Triglycerides (tag) 60–150 mg/dl

Q. What are the preservatives used in urine sample?

A. Formalin, thymol, chloroform, toluene, concentrated HCl and glacial acetic acid are the commonly used urine preservatives.

Q. What is the normal serum bilirubin level?

A. 0.2 to 1 mg/dl.

Q. What is the normal blood level of unconjugated bilirubin?

A. 0.2-0.6 mg/dl.

Q. What is the normal serum level of conjugated bilirubin?

A. Less than 0.2 mg/dl.

Q. What is latent jaundice?

A. Serum bilirubin between 1 mg/dl and 2 mg/dl.

Q. Jaundice appears at what level of bilirubin?

A. Jaundice appears if the serum bilirubin goes above 2 mg/dl.

Q. What is meant by van den Bergh.s direct positive test?

A. When bilirubin is conjugated, the purple colour is produced immediately on mixing with the reagent, the response is said to be van den Bergh.s direct positive.

Q. What is indirect positive van den Bergh.s test?

A. When the bilirubin is unconjugated, the colour is obtained only when alcohol is added, and this response is known as indirect positive.

Q. What type of bilirubin is present in hemolytic jaundice?

A. In hemolytic jaundice, unconjugated bilirubin is increased in serum. Hence van den Bergh.s test is indirect positive.

Q. What happens in obstructive jaundice?

A. In obstructive jaundice, conjugated bilirubin in serum is elevated, and van den Bergh.s test is direct positive.

Q. What about hepatocellular jaundice?

A. In hepatocellular jaundice, a biphasic reaction is observed, because both conjugated and unconjugated bilirubins are increased in serum.

Q. What are important liver function tests?

A. Serum bilirubin, albumin, alkaline phosphatase, urine bile salts, bile pigments and urobilinogen, Amino transferase S.G.P.T. and S.G.O.T.

Q. Increase in serum unconjugated bilirubin occurs in which condition?

A. Hemolytic jaundice.

Q. What are the features of obstructive jaundice?

A. Elevated conjugated bilirubin in plasma, presence of bile salts and bile pigments in urine, increased alkaline phosphatase level in blood, and increased cholesterol in blood.

Q. Which tests will be positive in a urine of a patient with obstructive jaundice?

A. Gmelin.s test, Hay.s test, and Fouchet.s test.

Q. What are the enzymes useful in diagnosis of liver diseases?

A. Alanine amino transferase, alkaline phosphatase, and gamma glutamyl transferase(ALT), Aspartate amino transferase(AST).

Q. What are the salient laboratory findings in a patient with chronic liver disease?

A. Serum albumin is lowered, albumin globulin ratio is reversed, and prothrombin time is prolonged.

Q. What is the characteristic laboratory findings in alcoholic cirrhosis?

A. Elevation of gamma glutamyl transferase level in serum.

Q. How much is glomerular filtration rate?

A. 120-125 ml per minute.

Q. What is the function of glomerulus?

A. An ultrafiltrate of the blood is produced in glomerulus, while the cells and proteins are retained in the blood.

Q. What is the normal renal threshold value for glucose?

A. Blood level of 180 mg/ dl.

Q. What is the normal specific gravity of urine?

A. 1.015 to 1.025.

Q. What is the minimum and maximum specific gravity of urine?

A. 1.003 to 1.032.

Q. What is the specific gravity of urine in chronic renal failure?

A. Fixed to 1.010.

Q. Specific gravity of urine increased in which condition?

A. Acute glomerulonephritis.

Q. Polyuria is seen in which conditions?

A. Diabetes mellitus, diabetes insipidus, and chronic renal failure.

Q. What are the features of chronic renal failure?

A. Urine with fixed specific gravity of 1.010, polyuria, increased blood urea and creatinine.

Q. Name abnormal substances seen in urine.

A. Protein, blood, sugar, ketone bodies, bile salts, bile pigments, and urobilinogen.

Q. Proteinuria is seen in which conditions?

A. Acute glomerulo nephritis, nephrotic syndrome, pyelonephritis, and multiple myeloma

Q. Which test is commonly employed to detect urinary protein?

A. Heat and acidification test.

Q. What is micro-albuminuria?

A. When small quantities of albumin (50-300 mg/ day) is seen in urine.

Q. How proteinurias are classified?

A. Glomerular proteinuria, overflow proteinuria, nephron loss proteinuria, tubular proteinuria, and urogenic proteinuria.

Q. What is meant by renal clearance?

A. Clearance is defined as the quantity of blood or plasma completely cleared of a substance per unit time and is expressed as milliliter per minute. It is the ml of plasma which contains the amount of that substance excreted by the kidney within a minute.

Q. How renal plasma flow is measured?

A. Para amino hippurate (Diodrast) clearance.

Q. What is the correct method for assessing glomerular filtration rate?

A. Inulin clearance.

Q. Haemoglobin is

A. Oligomeric protein and Chromoprotein

Q. Tryptophan is involved in the formation of

A. Vitamin Niacin and Indole Acetic Acid

Q. Which amino acid is not utilized by brain?

A. Glycine

Q. Glyoxysomes are concerned with metabolism of

A. Fats

Q. Which of the following phytohormone usually acts as bud inhibitor?

A. Indole Acetic Acid

Q. Which amino acids are NOT likely to be found on the outside regions of folded protein structures?

A. Hydrophobic amino acids

Q. Which of the following amino acids plays a role in redirecting the chain of amino acids when it folds into its tertiary structure?

A. Proline

Q. What is the major functional role of the zinc ion in the zinc finger?

A. Provides a point around which to fold a stable protein.

Q. What molecular forces contribute to the stabilization of protein structure?

A. Hydrophobic interactions, Electrostatic interactions (salt bridges), Disulfide bonds, Hydrogen bonds

Q. Zinc fingers have several arginine residues located at the bend between the alpha helix and the beta sheet. What function might these residues have in terms of the role that zinc fingers play in our cells?

A. Positively charged amino acids that interact with the negatively charged DNA

Q. Why is it important to design a protein that has only one stable protein structure?

A. If there are other ways to fold the protein, then the other folds will compete with the desired structure and spoil the construction. Have to have a protein design that is unstable in every other conformation and stable only in one.

Q. Why is the structure of Top7 so important in the quest to understand how proteins fold?

A. Scientists created an entirely new protein fold, and then using computational methods, designed a sequence of amino acids that they predicted would fold into this predicted structure. This is the first protein that was designed to fold a specific way.

Q. What is the advantage of learning to design protein structures?

A. Create proteins involved in biotechnology and medicine

Chapter 6 Virology

Q. Chemically Viruses called as?

A. Nucleoproteins

Q. The virus which attacks *E.coli* is termed as?

A. Coliphage

Q. First plant viruses were discovered in which plant?

A. Tobacco

Q. W.M. Stanley got Nobel Prize for:

A. Virus

Q. Prions are disease causing agents composed of:

A. Protein

Q. Western Blot test is used in the diagnosis of

A. AIDS

Q. What is the difference between swabs for viruses and bacteria?

A. Virus swab contain Viral transport media and antibiotics .

Q. Which virus belongs to rhabdovirus group that resembles a bullet, flat at one end?

A. Rabies

Q. Rabies source of specimen for virus isolation:

A. Saliva

Q. Colorado tick fever cultured on:

A. Blood

Q. Coxsackie specimen isolated on:

A. Throat swab + feces

Q. Influenza specimen isolated on:

A. Throat swab

Q. HSV specimen isolvated on:

A. Vessicle fluid

Q. A viral organism was isolated from a painful blister on the lip of a teenager girl. Agent was found to be double-stranded, linear DNA and was enveloped. The patient had similar sore 2 months ago:

A. Herpes Simples I (HSV)

Q. Cause of RSV

A. Cause of pneumonia and bronchiolitis in infants.

Q. The illness which often results infection with Poliovirus, Coxsackievirus and Echovirus is:

A. Aseptic meningitis

Q. Which strategy like to induce lasting intestinal mucosal immunity to poliovirus:

A. Oral vaccination OR live vaccine

Q. 9-month-old infant is brought to health dept. for second dose of OPV (oral polio virus) 2 weeks after 1st vaccine. Child has mild diarrhoea and decision is made to defer 2nd dose. Bacterial exam of stool is unremarkable but a small, single strand positive RNA virus is isolated. Same agent in sewage effluent previous week. Viral isolated not affected by either:

A. Poliovirus

Q. Varicella is:

A. Primary disease of children

Q. 6-months child with persistent cough + fever, physical exam and CXR suggests pneumonia. Which org is lease likely to cause infection:

A. Rotavirus

Q. A newborn infant has multiple, haemorrhagic cutaneous lesions and does not respond to SOUND. Head CT scan shows periventricular calcification:

A. Cytomegalovirus (CMV)

Q. Structural features of HIV including all Except:

A. Bullet-shaped virion

Q. The only hepatitis virus that can be grown *In vitro* is:

A. HAV

Q. Transmission is primarily by the fecal-oral route:

A. HAV

Q. Infected individuals do not become carriers:

A. HAV

Q. Male gender and early infancy are risk factors for chronic infection:

A. HBV

Q. Patient with jaundice. P/E reveals nodular, enlarged liver. CT of ab shows cirrhotic liver w/large mass. Ct-guided biopsy reveals malignant tumour derived from hepatic parenchymal cells:

A. HBV

Q. Hepatocellular carcinoma:

A. HBV/HCV

Q. Which hepatitis virus belongs to FLAVI virus group:

A. HCV

Q. Most infected persons become carriers:

A. HCV

Q. Autonomous replication as well as transmission from patient to patient can be accomplished by all Hepatitis viruses except:

A. HDV

Q. Transmission of this virus also have an active HBV infection:

A. HDV

Q. Child With sickle cell anemia/ She has been tired lately and may have come down with virus. She is very pale and severely anaemic. Bone marrow aspirate contains no erythroid precursor cells:

A. Parvovirus

Q. Virus measurement done by

A. Electron microscopy

Q. Viruses can only reproduce when inside a ____________________ cell.

A. living

Q. What was the first virus ever discovered?

A. Tobacco mosaic virus

Q. What type of molecule is the capsid surrounding the virus made of?

A. Protein

Q. What is the reproductive cycle of a phage virus called in which the virus's DNA is combined with the host cell's DNA to form a prophage?

A. Lysogenic cycle

Q. Which enzyme are retroviruses equiped with that allows them to transcribe DNA from an RNA template?

A. Reverse transcriptase

Q. What are the tiny molecules of naked circular RNA that infect plants called?

A. Viroids

Q. Which viruses has not a double strand linear DNA virus?

A. Papovavirus

Q. Which viruses has not a single strand linear RNA virus?

A. Bunyavirus

Q. Viroids differ from viruses in

A. Naked RNA molecules only

Q. Genetic material of retroviruses is

A. Single stranded RNA

Q. What consists of a nucleic acid genome packaged into a protein coat (capsid) or a Membrane (envelope)?

A. Virion

Q. Viruses with naked capsids (non-enveloped) are generally resistant to drying, acid, and detergents, including the acid and bile of the enteric tract. Many of these viruses are transmitted by the fecal-oral route and can endure transmission even in sewage.

A. True

Q. What viral replication step takes place after the attachment and penetration phase?

A. Un coating

Q. What is the phase in which an extracellular infectious virus symptoms is not detected?

A. Latent period

Q. A Jewish AIDS patient from Isreal presents to the ER with red-brown raised nodules on the lower limbs, face, and genitalia. Lymphodema is found upon palpation. The patient complains about difficulty eating and dark growths are found along the gum line. Which organism is the mostly likely cause?

A. Kaposi sarcoma-related virus (HHV-8)

Q. A 34-year-old kidney transplant patient currently on immunosuppressants complains of shortness of breath and coughing. Physical exam reveals fever and abnormal lung sounds while chest x-ray indicates interstitial infiltrates in the lungs. No cysts are detected on silver stain of bronchoalveolar lavage fluid, ruling out Pneumocysitic carinii infection. The doctor makes a diagnosis after viewing a sample of the patient's lung tissue, which shows abnormal giant cells. Which organism is the mostly likely cause?

A. Cytomegalovirus (CMV)

Immunology

Q. An organ represents a higher level of structure than the tissue composing it and performs functions that the tissues cannot peform alone. This is an example of the principle of

A. Emergent properties.

Q. The connection between structure and ________ is a basic concept of biology.

A. Function

Q. Stomata open when guard cells

A. Becomes more turgid because of an influx of K+ followed by the osmotic entry of water.

Q. Immunity definition

A. Resistance by the host towards injury caused by micro.org and/or products

Q. Types of immunity

A. Acquired - adaptive, Passive - natural, Local - destruction at local level, Herd - control of disease in body

Q. Measurement of immunity

A. Agglutination, Precipitation, Complement fixation, Testing level of antibodies

Q. Type of Immune Response:

A. Primary, Secondary, Humoral (Antibody mediated) response, Cellular (Cell mediated) response

Q. Immunogenicity depends on:

A. Foreignness, chemical nature/size

Q. Immune response altered by:

A. Amount of immunogen, time of exposure, mode of administration and duration of exposure

Q. Antigen/Antibody: response depends on:

A. Dose, route, timing, administration

Q. Antibodies:

A. Ab are produced in response to Ag, Abs are immunoglobulin's

Q. About IgG

A. Secondary response, Crosses placenta, Mainly in internal secretions (blood, CSF)

Q. About IgM

A. Primary response, Presence in fetus, intrauterine infection

Q. About IgA

A. Secretory immunoglobulin, Present in external secretions Tears, saliva, sweat, breast milk, GI secretions, Mucous secretion of respiratory tract, Urogenital tract.

Q. About IgD

A. Present in traces only, Found on surface of B lymphocyte, Marker for B mature cells

Q. About IgE

A. Allergic/antiparasitic responses

Q. Abnormal immunoglobulins

A. Cryoglubulins, Bence Jones proteins

Q. Names of Auto-immune diseases

A. Chronic thyroiditis + Grave's Disease, Hemolytic anaemia, Thrombocytopenia and granulocytopenia

Q. Immune deficiencies:

A. Abnormal immune response, Could be congenital or acquired, B-cell (Ab) – recurrent infections, T-cell – Acquired immuno deficiencies syndrome

Q. Location of B cells:

A. Follicles,

Q. Function of B cells:

A. Markers of foreign pathogen, antibody production.

Q. Location of T-cell:

A. Paracortex

Q. Function of T cells:

A. Defense against intracellular pathogens.

Q. Cells that attack (protozons):

A. CD4 T-cells

Q. ___ is responsible for B-cells activation

A. IL-1

Q. ___ is responsible for T-cells activation

A. C3

Q. ___ is responsible for Macrophages activation

A. Gamma-interferon from T-cells

Q. ___ is responsible for NK cells activation

A. Type II hypersensitivity reactions (kill tumor cells)

Q. ABO-incompatibility activation :

A. Transplant rejection/Type II hypersensitivity

Q. Rh blood group activation:

A. Only RBC's.

Q. Which cell recognize Class I antigen: (HLA-A/B/C)?

A. CD8 cytotoxic T-cells recognized these antigens

Q. Which cell recognize Class II antigen: (HLA-D)

A. CD4 helper T-cells and macrophage recognize these

Q. Requirement for success Transplantation

A. ABO blood group compatibility, Absence of anti-HLA cytotoxic Abs in recip, Close matches for HLA-A/B/D between donor/recipient, Transplant donors Siblings are best donors sources.

Q. Types of Graft

A. Autograft(Transfer of tissue from self-self, best survival), Isograft(Between identical twins), Allograft(Between unrelated individuals), Xenograft(Between one species to another (pig vavles))

Q. Latex agglutination reaction means:

A. Antibody to capsular antigen is attached to beads

Q. Example of Type-I hypersensitity reaction

A. Eczema, hives, asthma, hypersensitivity to bee sting (involves: IgE)(eryth. Lesions w/in 30min)

Q. Example of Type-II hypersensitity reaction

A. Goodpasture's syndrome, Myasthenia gravis, Cells coated by specific IgG/IgE Abs are destroyed by cells (eg: NK/esoinphils)

Q. Example of Type-III hypersensitity reaction

A. Serum sickness, SLE, Circulating immunocomplexs, IgG/IgM deposit in target tissue activate complement system

Q. Example of Type-IV (delayed type) hypersensitity reaction

A. Tuberculin, Dermatitis, Skin test needs to be perform

Q. In acute inflammation means

A. Accumulation of polymorh nuclear cells (PML)

Q. Patients deficient in C8 have increased incidence:

A. Meningitis due to *Neisseria*

Q. Inability to response to self-antigen also called as:

A. Tolerance

Q. HLA-27 is a risk factor for which disease?

A. Ankylosing spondylitis arthritis

Q. Which bacteria normally present in URT?

A. Normally gram positive shift to gram negative during disease.

Q. Define 'Infectious Disease'

A. A change from normal health or function of the host caused by a parasite or its products.

Q. A parasite that can cause an infectious disease is called a ___________?

A. Pathogen

Q. What is Virulence?

A. The extent of the pathogen's ability to cause disease.

Q. What are the 3 things that pathogens virulence depends on?

A. Establish a focus of infection spread to adjacent or other tissues cause morbidity by direct mechanical damage (disease)

Q. What is a reservoir?

A. Places where the pathogens normally live, multiply, and serve as a source of infection.

Q. List some different mechanisms of transmission:

A. Direct contact, indirect contact (fomites), Respiratory droplets

Q. What is a communicable disease?

A. Disease spread from one infected host to another (EX virus)

Q. What is a non-communicable disease?

A. Diseases caused by microorganisms that usually live outside the hose (EX fungi)

Q. What must bacteria do in order to establish a focus of infection?

A. Transmit an infectious dose from reservoir to portal of entry Compete with normal flora (adhesions, antibiotics, etc) Resist initial host defenses (leukocidins, phagocytosis, etc)

Q. What are the general systemic effects of an endotoxin?

A. Coagulation (DIC) Fibrinolysis (Haemorrhage) Complement activation.

Q. Why is collateral damage from host's response important?

A. There can be a pro-inflammatory and immunomodulatory cytokine 'storm' Inflammation can occur: vasodilatation, increased vascular.

Q. What is the major mode of transmission for *Staphylococcus*?

A. Enter wounds, teat orifaces, navel of newborns

Q. What are the disease patterns of *Enterococcus* bacteria?

A. Lower UTI Diarrhoea

Q. What is the treatment and control of *Enterococcus*?

A. Correct compromising conditions Topical polyantibacterials

Q. What are general points to remember for *Enterococcus* bacteria?

A. Diarrhoea!

Q. What are the histotoxic disease patterns of *Clostridium*?

A. Necrosis (blackleg, etc.), Wound infections, Septicemia

Q. What is the main treatment of *Clostridium* infections?

A. Antitoxins (counteract the toxins)

Q. *Actinomyces* is a member of the normal flora of what area on the body?

A. Normal flora of the upper respiratory tract (so DZ patterns are associated with that)

Q. Common signs with an *Escherichia* infection are?

A. Entero and non-toxigenic diarrhoea Invasive disease Endotoxemia

Q. Signs of *Salmonella* infections?

A. Diarrhoea, Septicemia, Pneumonia

Q. Name any one disease patterns of *Yersinia*?

A. Plague.

Q. Control/treatment for *Enterobacteriaceae* includes?

A. Vaccination.

Q. Treatment/control of Anaerobes?

A. Drain abscesses

Q. Example of antibiotic by inhibition of cell wall synthesis

A. Penicillin, Bacitracin, Vancomycin

Q. Example of antibiotic by inhibition of cell membrane function

A. Amphotreicin-B

Q. Example of antibiotic by inhibition of protein synthesis

A. Chloramphenicol, Tetracycline

Q. Example of antibiotic by inhibition of nucleic acid synthesis

A. Quinolones, Rifampin, Cirpo

Q. Half of the patients with allergic diseases have increased serum

A. IgE levels

Q. Antibody diversity is generated by

A. Allelic exclusion

Q. Hybridoma cells are

A. Non-anchorage dependent and can be grown in suspension culture

Q. Blocking of active site of an enzyme is a kind of

A. Competitive inhibition

Q. Difference between pathogenic and non-pathogenic enteric bacteria on basis of:

A. Lactose fermentation

Q. What is responsible for the outbreak of basically dysentery in rural area:

A. Human carrier

Q. Causes fever and inflammation:

A. Endotoxin

Q. Which enzyme activates the plasma plasminogen system:

A. Coagulase

Q. The tests based on the principle of toxin neutralization is/are

A. Schick test, Naglers reaction

Q. An example of Type I hypersensitivity reaction is

A. Casonis test

Q. Anaphylaxis is mediated by

A. Cytotropic antibodies

Q. Most widely accepted theory of antibody production is

A. Clonal selection theory

Q. A carrier who acquires the organism from another carrier is known as

A. A paradoxical carrier

Q. Adenosine deaminase (enzyme) deficiency is associated with:

A. Severe combined immunodeficiency (SCID) immunodeficiency (SCID)

Q. Carriers are not seen:

A. Measles

Q. IL-2 is secreted by:

A. CD4, lymphocytes and TH cells

Q. A chest physician performs bronchoscopy in the procedure room of the out patient department. To make the instrument safe for use in the next patient waiting outside, the most appropriate method to disinfect the endoscope is by:

A. 2% gluteraldehyde for 20min

Q. Neonatal thymectomy leads to:

A. Decreased size of paracortical areas

Q. IL-l produces

A. T lymphocytes activation(TH activation)

Q. Type of graft, best suited for renal transplantation:

A. Isograft

Q. Most common cause of chronic granulomatous disease in children is:

A. Defective H_20_2 production

Q. The numerous antibodies that provide immunity are proteins, whose specificity and diversity are achieved by:

A. Having large number of separate genes, each encoding separate antibody

Q. Match list-I (factors/enzyme) with list-II (activities) and select the correct answer using the codes given below the lists.

List-I (Factors/Enzyme)	List-II (Activities)
A. Sigma factor	1. Termition of transcription
B. Rho factor	2. Removal of RNA primer from newly synthesized
DNA strand	
C. DNA polymerase-I	3. Correct initiation of transcription
D. Amino-acyl synthetase	4. Correct initiation of DNA replication
	5. Attachment of amino acid to t-RNA

A. A-3, B- 1, C-2, D- 5.

Q. Which medicine is used in the treatment of AIDS?

A. Azidothymidine

Q. The organic compounds that contain nitrogen

A. Protein

Paracytology

Q. 27 yr IV drug user, diff swallowing. White plagues along tongue and oral mucosa budding yeast—

A. *Pseudohyphae*

Q. *Entamoeba histolytica* can cause:

A. Abscess in the liver and lungs

Q. What is the treatment of *cryptococcers neoformans*?

A. Amphoteran B – for cryptococal meningitis reaches CSF

Q. Healthy patient with contacts—dev ulcerative lesion of eye

A. *Acanthamoeba*—freshwater lakes

Q. 30yr old vet, usits ob exam—mild cervical lymphadenopathy, px-spiranycin—child beses of hydrocephalus cerebral calcification

A. *Toxoplasma gondi*

Q. Which of the following infections agents cannot complete its entire life cycle in the human without resorting to stages in other living organisms:

A. *Toxoplasma gondi*

Q. Which of the following statements are untrue of *pneumocystis carinii*:

A. Diagnosis is made by the serology; microscopy is of no value

Q. *Leishmania donovanum* produces:

A. Amastigotes which are seen in the human reticuloendothelial system

Q. A young child is admitted to your care. You find that he is anaemic with a very low lever of serum iron you order a stool specimen to be examined for ova and parasites. The laboratory informs you that the feces contains egg of Trichuris, Ascaris and Hookworm. The correct treatment would be:

A. Mebendazole and iron replacement

Q. The life cycle of which parasite involve being transmitted by drinking water containing copepods:

A. Dracunculus (Guinea worm)

Q. You are a paediatrician in Georgia and your patient has cholisretinitis of both eyes. You suspect he has an infection with Toxocara (cause of visceral larva migrans) which of the following is not an appropriate course of action for the physician to pursue:

A. Order of stool specimen to be examined for ova

Q. 45-yr-old male w/alcohol abuse, periodontal disease, fever/chills, pneumonia with lung consolidation. CXR shows cavity in right lower lung; what type of bacteria involved:

A. Anaerobic bacteria because organism is elsewhere + causing disease elsewhere (mixed infection)

Q. After handling deer pt. eats and experiences fever, non-productive cough, shortness of breath, lymphadenopathy and no skin lesions:

A. *Tularemia* due to handling animals

Q. Fever, chills, headache, myalgia, arthlargia. Ulcer with black base on right hand and epitrochlear lymphadenopathy. Patient knows to skin rabbits:

A. *Fanciella* (tularensis disease)

Q. Dairy farmer with fever, chills, myalgia, headaches, skin rash, vomiting. Spirochetes in blood. Early culture in serum shows enriched nutrient agar:

A. *Leptospira interrogans*

Q. Flea bites, rat infected shed, fever, chills, rash:

A. *Endermic typhus*—produced by rat fleas/ticks

Q. Tick bites—chronic arthritis, knee + hip + facial muscle weakness due to lyme disease. Which org:

A. *Erthema chronicum migrans*

Q. Which of the following organism has been associated with production of anemia in infected individuals:

A. *P. Vivax, N. Americana, D. Latum*

Q. Which of these parasite life cycle cannot be interrupted by sterilizing the feces of all infected people:

A. *Filariasis* (Heartworm-b/c transmitted thru mosquito bite)

Q. 33 yr pt. headache, blurred vision, phys exam= pupil edema + ataxia. Head CT scan

A. Non-dimorphic yeast. Found world wide

Q. Ohio river, headache, fever, malaise + non-productive cough after few days

A. Hishplasma capsulation

Q. Healthy pt. pusthetic, aortic valve post op fever, bld culture done

A. Broad spectrum antibiotics, 2 days later, shll febrole.

Biotechnology

Q. What are the four major areas of biotechnology?

A. Food and Consumer Goods, Agriculture, Medicine, and Environment

Q. What is the definition of biotechnology?

A. The use of cells and biological cells to make a product or solve a problem

Q. "New" biotechnology is based on changing organisms (living things) using what?

A. DNA

Q. Gregor Mendel is known as the father of which branch of science?

A. Genetics

Q. Which notable figure in the history of biotechnology is known as the Father of Medicine?

A. Hippocrates

Q. Which notable figures in the history of biotechnology are known for initiating (starting) the multibillion-dollar industry of biotechnology?

A. Stanly Cohen & Herbert Boyer

Q. Who produced early data critical to the discovery of DNA, but was not given credit for her work because she was a woman?

A. Rosalind Franklin

Q. Structure of DNA is discovering in which year?

A. 1953

Q. Who described the structure of DNA?

A. James Watson & Francis Crick

Q. Who headed the team that cloned Dolly using DNA from adult sheep cells and is know for ground-breaking research and is an expert on cloning?

A. Dr. Ian Wilmut

Q. Who created a vaccine for rabies and pasteurized milk to kill bacteria?

A. Louis Pasteur

Q. When did the word biotechnology first appear in print?

A. 1919

Q. What is the definition of the prefix bio?

A. Life, of living things

Q. When microbes are grown so that their amino acids can be used to produce a product such as Equal sweetner it is an example of:

A. Food and consumer goods

Q. Genetically altered crops that can grow in exceptionally dry or wet, hot or cold climates are an example of:

A. Agriculture

Q. Flu vaccine in the form of a nasal spray is an example of:

A. Medicine

Q. What is the role of promoter in gene expression?

A. It is site of recognition for transcription machinery.

Q. Which enzyme needed for making cheese?

A. Rennin

Q. What is the full form of NIH?

A. National Institute of Health

Q. Which software performs homology modelling?

A. SWISS-PDB Viewer

Q. Where are ribosomes located?

A. Cytoplasm

Q. What is the name of first cloned sheep?

A. Dolly

Q. What is the full form of EST's?

A. Expressed Sequencing Tags

Q. What can be the length of Primer?

A. 15 base pair

Q. Which chromosomes are the sex chromosomes?

A. X-chromosome and Y- chromosome

Q. BLAST and FASTA are used for

A. End free space alignment

Q. Which step is omitted in whole genome sequencing?

A. Making phage library

Q. The first product to be synthesised commercially through biotechnology was

A. Insulin

Q. All of the following are biotechnological processes used in medicine except:

A. Artificial intelligence

Q. A culture system with constant environmental conditions maintained through continual provision of nutrient and removal of wastes is called ____________ culture system.

A. Continuous

Q. A culture in a closed vessel to which no additional medium is added and from which no waste products are removed is called a ____________ culture.

A. Batch

Q. DNA sequences are stored in ________ for easy access.

A. Databases

Q. Sequences that share a common evolutionary ancestor are said to be

A. Homologous

Q. Describe the gel electrophoresis process.

A. It uses an electric current to separate various samples of DNA to different lengths in the gel. DNA fragments are attracted to the positive side of the pole. The larger the fragments the slower it migrates.

Genetics

Q. Enzymes involved in DNA replication:

A. 1. Nuclease 2. DNA polymerase 3. DNA ligase

Q. Type and function of nuclease.

A. 1. Exonuclease : break phosphor diaester bonds
2. Endonulease: attach on inner portion of one/double strend

Q. Type and function of DNA Polymerase.

A. 1. DNA Polymerase I
2. DNA Polymerase II
3. DNA Polymerase III
FUNCTION: carry polymerization

Q. Function of DNA Polymerase I

A. Role in polymerization and degradation process of nucleotide

Q. Function of DNA Polymerase II

A. It play role in repair synthesis

Q. Function of DNA Polymerase III

A. Main polymerization enzyme elongation

Q. Function of DNA ligase

A. Ligation of single stranded nicks in phosphodiester back bone

Q. Define: The Initiation codon :

A. Requires giving the signal to start protein synthesis.

Q. The initiation codon is:

A. AUG

Q. Define: The termination codon :

A. Requires giving the signal to stop protein synthesis.

Q. The termination codon are:

A. UAA, UAG, UGA

Q. Which Enzyme is require for PCR?

A. Taq polymerase

Q. The flow of genetic information from nucleic acid to protein is called

A. Transcription

Q. Which is the most successful vector in higher plants ?

A. Ti-plasmid

Q. About Conjugation:

A. Requires cell to cell contact, Plasmids are transferred, and Bacterial conjugation requires F-factor (Fertility)

Q. About Transduction

A. Phage mediated (infected bacteria), Virulent phage (assemble/ release new viruses), Temperature phage (may enter productive cycle or enter bacteria DNA and reside there)

Q. About Generalized Transduction

A. Do not require lysogeny and any gene may be transferred by infecting bacterial DNA

Q. The process by which RNA is formed from DNA is called

A. Transcription

Q. About Specialized Transduction

A. Requires lysogeny, only bacterial genes next to insertional site are transferred

Q. About Transformation

A. Uptake of donor DNA by recipient cells, most primitive mode of gene transfer

Q. What is Lysogenic conversion?

A. New properties are conferred on bacterial cell by products of prophage genes

Q. What is Bacterial Plasmids?

A. Carry genes for antibiotic resistance, carry genes for synthesis of pilli and genes that code for exotoxins, genes essential for growth of host cells are NOT carried

Q. In the 1940s, Barbara McClintock described 'Jumping genes' in maize. Such mobile segments of DNA, now called transposons can insert themselves:

A. Into virtually any part of any DNA molecule

Q. The enzymes that control the attachment of amino acids with t-RNA are

A. Synthetases

Q. Genomic library contains:

A. Cloned DNA stored *ex situ*

Q. The sheep 'Dolly' was created by:

A. Nuclear transplantation

Q. T/F The first gene to be Isolated was the lac operon of E. coli

A. TRUE

Q. T/F Restriction endonucleases can restrict infection of bacteria by bacteriophages by degrading the viral DNA

A. FALSE

Q. In a family, father and son were found to be colourblind. This is due to the defective recessive gene present in:

A. X-chromosome

Q. The first human hormone produced by recombinant DNA technology was:

A. Insulin

Q. The smallest unit of DNA which is capable of undergoing crossing-over and recombination is:

A. Recon

Q. Haemophilic gene of a father is inherited to:

A. All of his daughters

Q. A segment of DNA strand with base sequence of Adenine (A), Guanine (G), Cytosine (C), Thymine (T), Adenine (A), would give rise to the complementary strand of m-RNA with base sequence

A. U, C, G, A, U

Q. In protein synthesis, the enzyme that catalyses peptide bonding is located in the

A. Larger subunit of the ribosome

Q T/F Barbara McClintock recognized and named nucleolar organizers in the chromosomes.

A. False

Q. T/F Kennedy and Lehninger showed that the citric acid cycle, oxidative phosphorylation and fatty acid oxidation take place in mitochondria

A. TRUE

Q. T/F By the grafting experiments with Acetabularia, Hammerling firmly established the role of nucleus in heredity

A. TRUE

Q. Restriction-modification system of bacteria exists to:

A. Encourage recombination of new genetic material

Q. A sequence of nucleotides on DNA 'CATCATCATCAT' is changed through mutation to 'CAATCATCATCAT'. What is this type of mutation called?

A. Frame shift

Q. As an antibiotic inhibiting protein synthesis, what is the specific action of Rifamycin?

A. Denaturing RNA polymerase thereby blocking initiation at transcription

Q. Which microorganism's genome was first sequenced?

A. *Haemophilus influenzae*

Q. What is the field of genomic dealing with the sequence structure of DNA called?

A. Structural genomics

Q. What are cDNAs spots on a glass slide used for expression studies called?

A. Microarray

Q. What are linear DNA sequences or clones having overlapping sequences called?

A. Contigs

Q. Based on genomic studies, why do people say that different species and organisms had a common ancestor 100 million years ago?

A. The genome sequencing projects have revealed that the genomes of very different organisms e.g. mouse and man may be quite similar. 12% of the 18,000 worm genes encode proteins whose biological roles could be inferred from their sequence similarity to yeast genes and vice – versa i.e. almost a third of the 6000 yeast genes have functional equivalents in worm genes. It is estimated that the difference between human and chimpanzee genomes is only 1 to 3%. These similarities suggest that neither genome has changed much since we shared a common ancestor 100 million years ago.

Q. Differentiate between functional and structural genomics?

A. *Functional genomics*: This is a field of study which co-relates the structure and sequence of the genome to its function. In this field the information provided by structure genomics is used to study the function of genes or protein in a systematic manner.

Structural Genomics: In structural genomics, one studies the sequence-structure relationship of a genome. It represents an initial phase of genome analysis which involves creating high resolution genetic physical and transcript maps and ultimately sequencing the genome. Because of rapid advances in the field of proteomics the study of three dimension structure of all proteins has also become easier because of structural genomics.

Q. What causes genetic variations in individuals?

A. The genetic variations are caused due to single nucleotide polymorphisms or SNPs which can occur both in the coding and non-coding regions of the genome. It is believed that SNPs occur at 1.6 million to 3.2 million sites in the human genome and may affect gene function, depending upon exact base change and where it occurs.

Q. What is Human Genome Project?

A. The Human Genome project officially started on 1 Oct, 1990 in the United States, as a 15-year programme to map and sequence the complete set of human chromosomes, as well as those of general model organisms. The strategy of this international project was to make a series of maps of each human chromosome at increasingly finer resolution. In this approach chromosomes were divided into smaller fragments that could be cloned and fragments were arranged to correspond to their locations on a chromosome. After mapping, each of these ordered fragments would be sequenced.

Q. What are the reasons for completely sequencing a genome?

A. The reasons for completely sequencing a genome are:

(*a*) It provides a base for the discovery of all inventory of genes;

(*b*) The sequence shows the relationship between genes;

(*c*) It provides a set of tools for future experimentation;

(*d*) The sequencing provides an index to draw and organize all genetic information about the organism;

(*e*) Ultimately the whole genome sequence becomes an archive for further containing all the genetic information required to make the organism.

Q. What are the different areas which can be studied using microarray technologies?

A. This technique can be used to study the following areas:

(1) Tissue specific genomes

(2) Regulatory defects in a disease

(3) Cellular responses to environment

(4) Cell cycle variations

(5) Discovering drugs

Q. What is meant by SNP map? How many SNPs occur in the whole genome?

A. The position of SNPs on human DNA is depicted by SNP map. Around 1.6 to 3.2 million sites.

Q. Give example of one disease, whose susceptibility has been located with the help of SNPs.

A. Alzheimer's disease

Q. In which direction is the DNA sequences always read?

A. 5′− − − −→3′ directions

Q. What does the C-value paradox indicates?

A. The C-value paradox indicates that despite the increasing complexity in higher animals, the number of genes does not increase likewise.

Q. What are GMOs?

A. GMOs or genetically modified organisms are defined as organisms whose genetic characteristics are changed through genetic manipulation or modification.

Q. What is genetic modification?

A. Genetic modification is a technology used to alter genetic material of living cells or organisms in order to make them capable of producing new substances or perform new functions.

Q. How are GMOs produced?

A. They are produced through gene transfers, for example by transferring genes of desirable traits to agricultural crops.

Q. Which one is the pre-dominant DNA type in an animal cell?

A. B-DNA

Q. What is modern biotechnology?

A. Modern biotechnology means the transfer of genetic materials from one specie to the same specie or to another specie for purposes of modifying the characteristics of that species.

Q. What are other terms for modern biotechnology?

A. Modern biotechnology is also known as 'genetic engineering', 'genetic modification', 'gene technology' or 'gene splicing'.

Q. What are genetically modified foods (GMFs)?

A. Genetically modified foods mean foods that have been produced from or derived from or composed of organisms (include plants, animals and microorganisms) that have been genetically modified.

Q. What are the benefits of Agriculture biotechnology?

A. Biotechnology will bring environmental and agricultural benefits such as: Increase yields, improve the quality of seed grains, Increase levels of nutrients in certain crops, Reduces use of chemical pesticides, Energy savings and Reduce soil erosion.

Q. What are genes and where are they?

A. Genes or DNA in scientific language are chemical or nucleic acids that are one type of material that determine the characteristics of all living organisms. Genes are located in the nucleus of each cell of the body. Genes are the bodies that retain the characteristics that differentiate living organisms, in the form of an imprint of those characteristics. No living organisms have genes that make them exactly the same, thus making genes the key factor that distinguishes organisms.

Q. What is gene manipulation?

A. In the use of any technology that extracts genes from one organism for insertion into another organism, the result will be a change in the organism as it exists in nature. The technology used in gene manipulation or gene splicing is defined in scientific language as genetic engineering. The techniques used in genetic engineering have been used in biotechnology research for some time. However, at the present time, biotechnology is being modernized and is focussed on transgenic operations.

Q. What is the major component of the bacterial genome?

A. Double-stranded, circular DNA molecule

Q. How do bacterial cells divide and reproduce?

A. Binary fission

Q. How many bonds exist between G & C?

A. 3

Q. What is the direct transfer of genetic material between two bacterial cells that are temporarily joined?

A. Conjugation

Q. Okazaki fragments are associated with which essential process?

A. DNA replication

Q. One genus of bacteria that can be found in the bottom, black layer of a Winogradsky column is ___________.

A. Desulfovibrio

Q. Which type of plasmid, when taken up by a bacteria, confers the ability to create a sex pilus?

A. F-plasmid

Q. Which bond exists between Guanine and Cytosine?

A. Phosphodiester bond, Covalent bond, Hydrogen bond

Q. How many hydrogen bonds are their between Adenine and Thymine?

A. 2

Q. Who gave the Deoxyribonucleic Acid(DNA) model?

A. Watson and Crick

Q. What is Bt-cotton?

A. Cotton plant containing genes of Bt

Q. Which is a biofuel?

A. Bioethanol

Q. What is the structure of DNA?

A. Helical

Q. What is role of mRNA?

A. To carry the information decoded by DNA to ribosome

Q. Which structures contain genes for enzymes and antibiotic resistance?

A. Plasmid

Q. Lactose operon of Escherichia coli is

A. Inducible

Q. The terms cistron, recon and muton was proposed by

A. Benzer

Q. In Operon model, RNA Polymerase binds to

A. Promoter gene

Q. Transposon tagging is used to

A. Isolate a gene

Q. The frequency of spontaneous mutations is approximately

A. 10^{-6}

Q. Z DNA is characterized by

A. Left handed helix

Q. RNA Polymerase is inhibited by

A. Rifampicin & Actinomycin

Q. X rays cause mutation by

A. Changing the chromosome morphology

Q. The enzyme used in footprinting technique is

A. RNA polymerase

Q. DNA staining is done by

A. Feulgen staining

Q. Protoplast fusion can be achieved by

A. Polyethylene glycol

Q. Somatic hybridization is a

A. Asexual hybridization

Q. Transferases are involved in the transfer of

A. Phosphate group, amino group & Methyl group

Q. For the lyses of yeast cell wall, which enzyme is most commonly used?

A. Combination of Glucanases, Protease & Mannase.

Q. Volatile products can be separated by the process

A. Pervaporation

Q. Where do zinc fingers bind on the DNA?

A. Major groove

Q. Which portion of the alpha helix in the zinc finger contacts the DNA?

A. The amino-terminal portion

Q. What potential benefits can we gain from genetically modified foods?

A. Long shelf life, higher nutrient content & reduced chemical use

Q. Histones are rich in

A. Arginine and lysine

Q. A couple with normal vision had colourblind father each. What is the percentage of probability that the daughter of the couple is colourblind?

A. 25%

Q. Which types of specialized sequences are carried at both ends of linear chromosomes for faithful DNA replication, ageing and maintaining polarity?

A. Repetitive sequence

Q. Sickle cell anaemia is due to the substitution of:

A. Valine for glutamic acid at 6th position in 13-chain

Q. Philadelphia chromosome refers to the translocation between the long arms of:

A. Chromosomes 9 and 22

Q. A form of chromosomal aberration that involves the fusion of long arms of acrocentric chromosomes at the centromere is known as:

A. Robertsonian translocation

Q. The ineffectiveness of many antibiotics to bacteria today is most closely associated with:

A. R-plasmid

Q. In DNA, the deoxygenation is at:

A. Second carbon atom

Q. An antibiotic that resembles the 32 end of a charged t-RNA molecule and brings premature termination of protein synthesis is

A. Puromycin

Q. Who discovered Polymerase Chain Reaction (PCR)?

A. Kary Mullis

Q. Full name of R.F.L.P.

A. Restriction Fragment Length Polymorphisms

Q. Full name of A.F.L.P.

A. Amplified Fragment Length Polymorphisms

Q. Full name of R.A.P.D.

A. Random Amplification of Polymorphic DNA

Q. Full name of S.S.P.

A. Single strand conformation polymorphism

Q. What do EST stands for?

A. Expressed Sequence Tags

Plant Tissue Culture

Q. Who proposed the concept of the 'cell theory'?

A. The cell theory was proposed by Schleiden and Schwann.

Q. Define Cell-totipotency.

A. It is defined as the ability of a plant cell to regenerate into whole plant.

Q. What is the basic technique in plant tissue culture?

A. The property of cell totipotency is exploited to culture the plant cells.

Q. Which is the most commonly used culture medium for plant cells and tissues?

A. The most extensively used nutrient medium is MS medium which was developed by Murashige and Skoog in 1962.

Q. Name the substance added to the culture medium to induce callus induction.

A. Auxins

Q. With reference to the enzymes in mitochondria, match list-I (location in mitochondria) with list-II (enzymes) and select the correct answer using the code given below the lists:

List-I (Location in mitochondria)	List-II (Enzymes)
A. Outer membrane	1. Adenylate kinase
B. Inner membrane	2. Fatty acid Co-A ligase
C. Inter-membranal space	3. Malate dehydrogenase
D. Matrix	4. Succinic acid dehydrogenase

A. A2 B 4 C 1 D 3

Q. Which one of the following is a major green house gas?

A. CO2

Q. Why The pulp of the pear fruit is hard,?

A. because of the presence of sclereids

Q. Pedology refers as an?

A. To the study of soil

Q. Which is impotant element of chlorophyll?

A. Magnesium

Q. Define 'callus'

A. Callus is referred as undifferentiated mass of tissues

Q. A plant cell is distinguished from an animal cell

A. It distinguished by the presence of cell wall

Q. Who introduces binomial nomenclature?

A. Linnaeus

Q. The five kingdom concept was proposed by

A. Whittaker

Q. Hydroponics means:

A. Plant growth in liquid culture medium

Q. Red tides are causd by

A. Red dinoflagellates

Q. 'Tikka' disease is found in which plant?

A. Groundnut

Q. Who is the well known Indian paleobotanist?

A. Birbal Sahni

Q. Give the example of smallest flowering plant

A. Wolffia

Q. Symbolic nitrogen fixation is done by

A. Rhizobium

Q. Lack of which element makes the plant insectivorous?

A. Nitrogen

Q. Who is the founder of binomial nomenclature?

A. Cark Linnaeus

Q. Laminaria is an important source of which product?

A. Iodine

Q. Define 'Donann equilibrium'

A. A theory which explains the physiological phenomenon is called mineral absorption

Q. Litmus is obtained from

A. An algae

Q. Bacteria which convert atmospheric nitrogen into nitrates they are called as?

A. Denitrifying bacteria

Q. With what technology do you associate 'callus' with?

A. Pollen analysis

Q. Which one of the following is a climax forest?

A. Thorn forest

Q. What is the first stable product of photosynthesis?

A. Sugar

Q. Use of Ganong's photometer

A. Ganong's photometer is used to measure the loss of water by plants

Q. An interaction between non-allelic genes in which an allele at one locus prevents expression of an allele at another locus but not *vice versa*, is called:

A. Epitasis

Q. Name a few compounds used as cryoprotectants.

A. Dimethyl sulfoxide (DMSO), glycerol, peoline and mannitol.

Q. Name the bacteria known as natural genetic engineer of plants

A. Agrobacterium tumefaciens is the bacteria known as natural genetic engineer of plants.

Q. What is the name of the first inter-genetic somatic hybrids between potato and tomato?

A. The first inter-genetic somatic hybrids between potato and tomatoes are known as 'Pomatoes' or 'Topatoes'.

Q. -------- is the gas responsible for the ripening of fruits.

A. Ethylene

Q. Golden rice is rich in -----------

A. Pro-vitamin A

Q. ----------refers to an unorganized mass of cells, which are generally parenchymatous in nature.

A. Callus

Q. Breeding associated with molecular markers (nucleic acid) is known as ----------

A. Molecular Breeding

Q. Genetically engineered ------ plants produced polyhydroxy butyrate globules in their chloroplasts.

A. Arabidopisis

Q. ---------- is the enzyme which inhibits pollen formation and hence prevents unnecessary pollination.

A. Barnase

Q. What are the uses of callus culture?

A. Callus cultures are used for:

(*a*) Plant regeneration

(*b*) Preparation of single cell suspensions and protoplasts

(*c*) Genetic transformations studies

Q. Write some uses of cell suspension cultures?

A. The cell suspension cultures are used for:

(*a*) Induction of somatic embryos/shoots

(*b*) *In vitro* mutagenesis and mutant selection

(*c*) Genetic transformation

(*d*) Production of secondary metabolites

Q. Define 'Explant culture'

A. *Explant Culture:* The culture of the plant parts (explants) is known as explant culture. The explants can be any part of the plant like the piece of stem, leaf, cotyledon, hypocotyls etc.

Q. Define 'Callus culture'

Callus culture: Callus refers to an unorganized mass of cells, which are generally parenchymatous in nature. Callus cultures are used for plant regeneration, preparation of single cell suspensions and protoplasts, and genetic transformations.

Q. What do you mean by *in vivo* gene banks and *in vitro* gene banks?

A. *In vivo* gene banks have been made to preserve the genetic resources by conventional methods *e.g.* seeds, vegetative propagules etc. *In vitro* gene banks have been made to preserve the genetic resources by non-conventional methods is cell and tissue culture methods. This ensures the availability of valuable germplasm to breeder to develop new and improved varieties.

Q. What is the technique of parasexual hybridization?

A. The parasexual hybridization or somatic cell hybridization offers an alternative for obtaining distant hybrids with useful agronomic traits (known as somatic hybrids or parasexual hybrids) which would never be formed in nature through sexual fertilization. The protoplast is isolated from the two sources and is allowed to randomly fuse with each other. The required fusion products are selected either through visual selection, biochemical methods, and fluorescent dyes.

Q. What are the natural secondary metabolites produced from plants?

A. Plants produce thousands of sophisticated chemical molecules. These include the chemicals that are required for the plant's basic metabolic processes such as alkaloids, resins, tannins, latex etc. Shikonin is obtained from Lithospermum erythrohizon is used as antimicrobial, red pigment used in lipsticks and dye for silk. Quinine is obtained from Cinchonal officinalis is used as antimalarial drug.

Q. "The Agrobacterium is considered as Natural Genetic engineer of plants." Comment.

A. This bacterium is known as natural genetic engineer of plants since these bacteria have the natural ability to transfer T-DNA of their plasmids into plant genome upon infection of cells at the wound site and cause an unorganized growth of a cell mass known as crown gall. Ti Plasmids can be used as gene vectors for delivering useful foreign genes into target plant cells and tissues. The foreign gene is cloned in the T-DNA region of Ti – plasmid in place of unwanted sequences.

Q. What is direct gene transfer?

A. In the direct gene transfer methods, the foreign gene of interest is delivered into the host plant cell without the help of a vector.

Q. Discuss in detail: 'Chemical mediated Gene transfer'

A. Certain chemicals like polyethylene glycol (PEG) and dextran sulphate induce DNA uptake into plant protoplasts.

Q. Discuss in detail 'Microinjection'

A. Here the DNA is directly injected into plant protoplasts or cells using fine tipped glass needle or micropipette.

Q. Discuss in detail 'Electroporation'.

A. In this case, a pulse of high voltage is applied for protoplasts/cells/tissues, which makes transient pores in the plasma membrane which facilitates the uptake of foreign DNA.

Q. Discuss in detail 'Particle Gun'.

A. In this method, the foreign DNA is coated (precipitated) on to the surface of minute gold or tungsten particles (1-3 micrometer) and bombarded (shot) on to the target tissue or cells using a particle gun (also called as gene gun/shot gun/micro projectile gun).

Q. What is the specialty of the plant bioreactor?

A. Plant cells are cultured in specially designed 'plant bioreactors' which essentially do not have a stirrer because plant cells are shear sensitive. In place of stirrer, gas is gently bubbled which provides stirring as well as meet the demand of a higher oxygen supply.

Q. What is Golden Rice? In what way it is different from the normal rice?

A. Normal rice is very low in vitamin *A*. Prof. Ingo Potrykus and Dr. Peter Beyer developed genetically engineered rice known as Golden rice which is enriched in pro-vitamin A by introducing three genes involved in the biosynthetic pathway for carotenoid, the precursor for vitamin *A*. The seeds of Golden rice are yellow in color because of pro-vitamin A which is produced in the entire grain.

Q. What is the name of the first genes available for genetic engineering of crop plants for pest resistance?

A. The first genes available for genetic engineering of crop plants for pest resistance were 'cry genes' (popularly known as Bt genes) from a bacterium Bacillus thuringensis.

Q. What is biotechnology?

A. Biotechnology is broadly defined as the use of biological processes of microbes, and of plants or animal cells to develop new products for the benefit of humans.

Q. What are Bt crops?

A. Bt crops are crops genetically engineered to carry the gene from the soil bacterium *Bacillus thuringiensis*. The bacteria produces a protein that is toxic when ingested by certain Lepidopteran insects. Crops containing the Bt gene are able to produce this toxin, thereby providing protection throughout the entire plant.

Q. What is Bt cotton?

A. Bt cotton is genetically engineered cotton to control tobacco budworms, bollworms, and pink bollworms.

Q. What are Herbicide-tolerant crops?

A. Crops that were developed to survive certain herbicides that previously would have destroyed the crop along with the targeted weeds, and allow farmers to use them as post-emergent herbicides, providing an effective weed control. The most common herbicide-tolerant crops (cotton, corn, soybeans, and canola) are Roundup Ready (RR) crops resistant to glyphosate, a herbicide effective on many species of grasses, broadleaf weeds, and sedges.

Q. What are Transgenic plants?

A. They are resulted from the insertion of genetic material from another organism so that the plant will exhibit a desired trait. Recombinant DNA techniques (DNA formed by combining segments of DNA from different organisms) are usually used.

Q. What is plant breeding?

A. Plant breeding is the use of techniques involving crossing plants from the same or closely related species to produce varieties with particular characteristics (traits) which are carried in the genes of the plants and passed on to future generations. It combines all the genetic traits of the two plants. Thus, there may be some undesirable traits in the offspring plant. Plants with the desired characteristics are then selected for breeding. The ability to obtain the desired features is dependent on chance. This process is very time-consuming and does not always result in a desirable plant.

Q. What is plant biotechnology?

A. Plant biotechnology is the addition of selected traits to plants to develop new plant varieties. It is an improvement on traditional plant breeding. For centuries, farmers have worked to develop new crops that will provide better yields and better quality foods. Biotechnology allows the plant breeder a wider choice of traits to chose from and allows the trait to be realized in a more precise manner and within a shorter time period. Plant biotechnology offers an additional, more accurate, sustainable method to improve the yield of existing farmlands and produce a more abundant food supply.

Q. How are the new plants different from the existing ones?

A. Plants developed through biotechnology carry specific genetic traits or characteristics that would be difficult or impossible to acquire using traditional plant breeding practices. Plant biotechnology makes it possible to transfer a single desired trait from any organism to a plant.

Q. What kind of plants result from plant biotechnology?

A. Plant biotechnology allows for the transfer of one or a few desired genetic traits without undesirable traits. For example, researchers are developing plants with a built-in protection against a specific insect, a built-in protection against a specific plant disease, a built-in tolerance to a specific herbicide (weed killer), improved nutrient content, and a number of other beneficial traits.

Q. A plant cell placed in hypotonic solution will

A. Swell up and become turgid

Q. Chemotropic movement is shown by

A. Pollen tube

Q. Movement of phloem sap from a sugar source to sugar sink

A. May translocate sugars from the breakdown of stored starch in a root up to developing shoots.

Q. The productivity of a crop declines when leaves begin to wilt mainly because

A. Stomata close, preventing CO2 from entering the leaf.

CHAPTER 12

Animal Tissue Culture

Q. Which antigen is present on T-cells which cause graft rejection during transplantation?

A. Surface antigen CD3 exposed on mature T-lymphocytes is responsible for allograft rejection.

Q. How does OKT3 help in transplantation?

A. An antibody directed against CD3 surface antigen of T –cells, OKT3 (anti-CD3 Moab) removes antigen bearing cells from circulation and from the graft.

Q. Which are the most commonly used enzymes for separating cells in a given tissue for culture?

A. Trypsin and collagenase

Q. Which is the first drug to be produced by mammalian cell culture?

A. Tissue plasminogen Activator

Q. What do you mean by cell based therapy?

A. The stem cell technology is used to replace damaged and dead cells to treat blood cancer, neuro and degenerative diseases etc. This is known as cell based therapy.

Q. Name a few medically important commercial proteins produced by animal cell culture.

A. t-PA protein produced by CHO cells is used to treat heart attack.
Factor VIII from CHO cells is used to treat Haemophilia A.
FSH From CHO cells is used to treat fertility.

Q. What is the most distinct feature of animal cell culture?

A. Animal cells can grow in simple glass and plastic containers. While growing microbial cells and plant cells, if the nutritive medium is changed and the cells are replenished with the culture medium, the cells will grow indefinitely. However, animal cells, depending on the tissue they have been isolated from can grow even in the best nutritive media to only limited generations. The animal cells in culture also exhibit contact inhibition.

Q. ------- was the first drug to be produced by mammalian cell culture.

A. Tissue plasminogen activator

Q. ------- are used for scaling up the production of suspension cells.

A. Spinner cultures

Q. In------ the cells adhere to the total curved surface of the microcarrier beads.

A. Roller bottles

Q. An------- microscope is used for visualizing cell cultures in situ.

A. Inverted microscope

Q. -----------involves the storing of cells at very low temperature.

A. Cryopreservation

Q. ------------is a highly effective therapeutic agent who reverses acute renal allograft rejection.

A. OKT3

Q. -----------play a major role in rejecting foreign tissue in transplantation.

A. T cells

Q. The animal cells in culture exhibit the phenomenon of -------

A. Contact inhibiton

Q. The maintenance of growth of the cells in culture medium is known as ----------

A. Primary cell culture

Q. ---------- are those cell lines which have a limited life span and they grow through a limited number of cell generations.

A. Finite cell lines

Q. Cell lines transformed under *in vitro* culture conditions give rise to – – – – – – – – – –

A. Continuous cell line

Q. What is a chimeric mouse?

A. Embryonic stem cells are cell lines directly derived from the inner cell mass of fertilized mouse embryo with out the use of immortalizing or transforming agents. It fertilized mouse egg is grown in culture (in vitro fertilization), it is observed that after several steps of cleavage, the cells which are dividing get accumulated in one corner. These cells are called inner cell mass (ICM cells) cells. These cells could be maintained in tissue culture in the presence of irradiated fibroblast cells. It was observed that these cells could be used to create chimeric mice. In chimeric mice, it was possible to take ES cells from a black mouse and implant it into the embryo of an albino (white) mouse. The progeny so developed had skin colour of black and white (a chimera).

Q. What are the differences between plant cell culture and animal cell culture?

A. The plant cells in culture can grow indefinitely if the nutritive media is constantly replenished. However, the animal cells, depending on the tissues they have been isolated from can grow even in the best nutritive media to limited generations. The animal cells also exhibit contact inhibition i.e. when cells grow and reach the walls of the container they are prevented from further growth. Another important feature of cell growth in culture is that their environment is different from that in vivo. The other major differences include the absence of cell-cell interaction, cell-matrix interaction etc.

Q. What is Embryonic stem cell culture?

A. Embryonic stem cells are cell lines derived directly from the inner cell mass of fertilized mouse embryo without use of immortalizing or transforming agents. If we fertilized a mouse egg and grow it in tissue culture, it is observed that after several steps of cleavage, the cells which are dividing get accumulated in one corner. These cells are called inner cell mass (ICM) cells. These cells could be maintained in tissue culture in the presence of irradiated fibroblast cells. These cells could retain the characteristics of the embryo founder cells, even after prolonged culture and extensive manipulation. The cells reintegrate fully into embryogenesis when returned to the early embryo. The cells would be used to create chimeric mice and to maintain a stable euploid karyotype. The cells would renew without differentiating in culture.

Q. Define 'Finite cell lines'

A. Finite cell lines are those cell lines which have a limited life span and they grow through a limited number of cell generations. Finite cell lines show the property of contact inhibition, density limitation and anchorage dependence. The mode of growth is in the monolayer form. The growth rate is slow and doubling time is around 24 to 96 hrs.

Q. Define 'Continuous cell lines'

A. Cell lines transformed under *in vitro* culture conditions give rise to continuous cell lines. The various properties associated with continuous cell lines are, the ploidy—either aneuploid or heteroploid. There is no contact inhibition and no anchorage dependence. The mode of growth is either monolayer or suspension form. The growth rate is rapid and doubling time is 12 to 24 hours.

Q. What do you understand by the term hybridoma technology?

A. Antibodies obtained from serum are a heterogeneous population of proteins released by different populations of B lymphocytes and therefore are known as polyclonal antibodies and bind very specifically to an epitope or an antigen. They are produced from antigen activated B lymphocytes cells that have been immortalized by hybridizing (fusing) them with a myeloma cell (cancerous lymphocyte). Ceaser, Milstein and George Kohler developed the immortalized hybridoma cell line by fusion of antibody producing B cells and cancerous cell (myleoma) in presence of polyethylene glycol (PEG). Thus the hybrid retains the ability of the B cells to secrete antibody and the ability of the myeloma cell to grow indefinitely. The Hybridoma technology has created a revolution in the area of diagnostics and antibody based therapy.

Q. What is the importance of karyotyping in established cell lines?

A. Once a cell has been established, its karyotype is determined. This will confirm the species of origin, at least for those cells karyotyped, and determine the extent of gross chromosomal changes in the line. Karyotypes may vary from being near normal tobeing aneuploid. While a normal karyotype is desirable, the presence of an abnormal karyotype is desirable, the presence of an abnormal karyotype does not preclude using the cells for in vitro studies, especially if it has been demonstrated that the cells retain the normal function expected of them.

If a normal karyotype is required *e.g.* to create transgenic animals, then special care is taken in handling the cells to minimize chromosomal changes. The stability of the karyotype depends on the species from which they are derived, the growth conditions used, the way in which the cells are subcultured, and whether or not the cells are frozen.

Q. Differentiate between roller bottle and spinner cultures?

A. In roller bottles the cells adhere to the total curved surface area of the microcarrier beads, thereby markedly increasing the available space for growth. These tissue culture bottles can be used in specialized CO2 incubators with attachments that rotate the bottles along the long axis. After each complete rotation of the bottle, the entire cell monolayer has transiently been exposed to the medium. The volume of the medium need only be sufficient to provide a shallow covering over the monolayer.

Spinner Cultures: Spinner cultures are used for scaling up the production of suspension cells. They consist of a flat surface glass flask with a suspended central Teflon paddle that turns and agitates the medium when placed on a magnetic stirrer. Commercial versions incorporate one or more side arms for sampling and/ or decantation. The cells are not allowed to settle to the bottom of the flask and thus cell crowding occurs only at very high densities.

Q. What is the use of microcarrier beads?

A. The microcarrier beads are used to increase the number of adherent cells per flask and are either dextran or glass based . they come in a range of densities and sizes. The beads are buoyant and therefore can be used with spinner culture flasks. The surface area available for cell growth on these beads in huge.

Q. What functions are performed by LAF? How many types of LAFs are present?

A LAF hood (Laminar Air flow hood) perform two functions:

(*i*) to protect the tissue culture from contamination by protecting it from the operator (*i.e.* Sterile environment);

(*ii*) to protect the operator from the tissue culture (in situation of potential infection risk).

Depending on the nature of the cells and organisms being handled three types of culture hoods are available:

Class I hoods give good protection to the operators and to a lesser degree, the cell culture.

Class II hoods offer protection to both the operator and the cell culture.

Class III hoods are used for work with highly pathogenic organisms.

Q. What are the drawbacks of using primary cell cultures?

A. The drawbacks of primary cell culture are that they are time consuming and require use of line animals or fresh tissue. Also there can be considerable variation from one preparation to another particularly if prepared by different people. These difficulties can be overcome by using secondary cell cultures.

Q. What are the advantages of using established cell lines for research by the scientists?

A. The advantages of using established cell lines is that their growth characteristics, media requirements and responses to selected reagents are established and therefore convenient for the scientist to use.

Q. Which one is the pre-dominant DNA type in an animal cell?

A. B-DNA

CHAPTER

13

Bioinformatics

Q. What is bioinformatics?

A. Bioinformatics is the management and analysis of biological information stored in data bases especially in late 1980's when researchers started to use computers as central sequence repository, from where the data could be accessed remotely.

Q. What is Ref Seq?

A. Ref Seq is a well verified database of mRNAs and proteins of human, mouse and rat. The data provided in Ref Seq has been used in many cases such as designing gene chips and describing the sequence features of the human genome.

Q. What is the BLAST family of search tools?

The 'BLAST' acronym stands for Basic Local Alignment Search Tool. A given sequence in the database using matrices that specify scores to either 'reward' a match or 'penalize' a mismatch. Top scoring matches are ranked to distinguish between a similarity due to ancestral relationship or due to random chance. True matches are further examined thoroughly with other details accessible through Entrez and other tools available at NCBI.

Q. What are the differences between directed and random sequencing?

A. *Directed Sequencing of BAC Contigs:* BAC vectors are capable of carrying inserts as large as 80-100 Kb. The vectors are used to make Genomic Libraries. The overlapping regions are used to assemble the various insets into continuous contigs. The individual contigs are then sequenced by breaking the DNA and cloning into smaller vectors. Since this is a stepwise directed method it is also called as Directed sequencing.

Random Shotgun Sequencing: In this method the genome is randomly broken up into sizes of 2-10 kb range and inserted into a vector (plasmids). These are then sequenced and ordered with respect to each other with the help of overlapping or common sequences.

Q. What are database retrieval tools and what are its uses?

A. Among the database retrieval tools are ENTREZ, taxonomy, BROWSER, LoCUS LINK. Entrez is an integrated database retrieval system. Through this system one can access literature (in the form of abstracts), sequences, and structures. Entrez is an excellent system for obtaining comprehensive information on a given biological question. The taxonomy browser provides information on taxonomic classification of various species.

Q. Mention all the databases and the type of information available on them?

A. Database Information available

EMBL (European Molecular Biology Laboratory) Nucleotide sequence

SWISS-PROT Annotated protein sequence

PDB (Protein Database) Three-dimensional structure of proteins

Ribosomal RNA database rRNA subunit sequences

PALI database Phylogenetic analysis and alignment of proteins

Q. What are the different types of sequences entered into the databases?

A. Based on their origin the various DNA sequence entries into the databases can be classified into the following types:

cDNA: Many sequences entered are originally cDNA sequences. While entering such sequences one has to mention this fact. Also this information is available when the sequence is retrieved. Thus these are expressed as part of the total sequences.

Genomic DNA: Most sequences entered are Genomic DNA sequences.

ESTs: Stands for Expressed Sequence Tags. These comprises of partial cDNA clones *i.e.* cDNAs sequence from one end. It has its own special database called the db EST. EST data can give information regarding the expression patterns by counting the number of ESTs corresponding to each gene divided by the total number of ESTs.

GST: In Plasmodium falciparum the enzyme Mung Bean nuclease cuts between the genes. The digested DNA can be used to prepare genomic library. The sequence can be read from either ends as in ESTs.

Organelle DNA: Eukaryotic cell possess cell organelles such as mitochondria, chloroplast. Since they possess their own DNA which is different from the Genomic DNA one has to mention it specifically while entering such data.

Other molecules such as tRNA and smaller RNAs are also entered into databases.

Q. Tell me about the different kinds of DNA sequences.

A. There are three kinds of DNA sequences. Genomic DNA comes from the genome and includes both genes and extragenic material. cDNA is reverse transcribed from mRNA and corresponds only to the expressed parts of the genome. Recombinant DNA is man-made and is composed of artificial DNA.

Q. If you had 1,500 base pair pieces of random DNA and you wanted to know how many of them had homology to known genes, what would you do to determine that?

A. I would use a BLASTX search against a known protein database - such MCBI's NR database. I would then sort them to determine how many were unique.

Q. What technique is used to measure the number of copies of a gene or an RNA molecule in human tissues?

A. PCR or polymerase chain reaction in real time, as opposed to the conventional method, because the number of copies of the target molecule can be monitored for each PCR cycle.

Q. What are the limitations of blotting techniques and what alternatives can you suggest?

A. The major limitation of blotting procedures is the length of time needed and the fact that they can accommodate only one probe at a time. DNA microchip technology permits the analysis of thousands of genes at the same time. DNA molecules are attached to the wafers in an organized array and are called the probes. DNA molecules taken from tissues are hybridized to the chips and are called targets, which are labeled with fluorescent light. The probes that have hybridized to the fluorescent targets are then identified by fluorescence microscopy.

Q. What technique is used to measure the number of copies of a gene or an RNA molecule in human tissues?

A. PCR or polymerase chain reaction in real time, as opposed to the conventional method, because the number of copies of the target molecule can be monitored for each PCR cycle.

Q. What kinds of analysis can be done using bioinformatics tools?

A. Many kind of analysis can be made using various bioinformatics tools. These are as follows:

(*a*) *Processing raw information*: The bioinformatics tools are used to process the experimentally determined sequence/raw information into genes, the proteins encoded with their functions, the regulatory sequences, and inferring phylogenetic relationships;

(*b*) *Genes*: Gene prediction can be done by using computer programmes like GeneMark for bacterial genomes and GENSCAN for eukaryotes;

(*c*) *Proteins*: Simple computer programmes are used to infer protein sequences from the predicted genes;

(*d*) *Regulatory sequences:* Bioinformatics tools can be used to analyse and identify the regulatory sequences;

(*e*) *Inferring phylogenetic relationships*: Information regarding the relationships between organisms can be obtained by aligning multiple sequences, calculating evolutionary distance, and constructing phylogenetic trees;

(*f*) *Making a Discovery*: Using the bioinformatics tools and databases, the functions of unknown genes can be predicted.

Q. Who discovered the EST technique?

A. Craig Venter and his research group.

Q. ––––––– is a government issued document that provides the holder the exclusive rights to manufacture, use or sell an invention for a defined period.

A. Patent

Q. ––––––––– relates to work of literary or artistic craftsmanship, engineering drawings and software.

A. Copyright

Q. –––––––– relates to distinctive words or symbols applied to products or services.

A. Trademark

Q. The structure of a patent has two parts–––––––– and––– ––––.

A. Description, Claims

CHAPTER 14

Bacteriological Examination of Pathogenic Bacteria

Name of organism: *Staphylococcus aureus* (virulent) (non-motile, non-sporeforming, facultative anaerobe) Gm+ cocci

Diseases	Characteristics	Habitat	Pathogenesis	Diagnosis
1	2	3	4	5
Skin infections:* impetigo, cellulitis, erysipelas, abcess, furuncle, carbuncle **Bacteremia/ sepsis:* hematogenous spread **Acute endocarditis*: **DESTRUCTIVE (compare to *S.viridans* and *S.faecalis*) **Pneumonia* – damaging	Gm + cocci in grapes/clusters Catalase + coagulase +	Ubiquitous in environment; normal flora of skin/ nose Spread through lesions, Fomites	*Enterotoxin*- vomiting, diarrhoea, heat resistant, (actually released in gut) *TSST-1* – tampon use, wounds, superantigen Exfoliatin- scalded skin *TISSUE SPREAD: Alpha toxin (lechthinase)*- Skin necrosis;hemolysis *Hyaluronidase*- degrades proteoglycans *Fibrinolysin*- lysis fibrin clots	Gm + cocci in grapes, Catalase differentiates from Strep. *S.aureus*: Beta hemolysis, coagulase, Yellow (Au) pigment (coagulase causes coagulation!) Coagulase neg: *S. epidermidis*: novobiocin sensitive "sensitive skin"

(Contd...)

1	2	3	4	5
process, cavitations, empyema, effusions **Osteomyelitis/ septic arthritis*- hematogenous and traumatic spread **Food poisoning* – 1-8 hr. onset, vomiting, preformed toxin **Tox shock syndrome* fever, vomiting, diarrhea, diffuse erythematous rash			*IMMUNE EVASION:* *Protein A*- binds IgG-Fc, blocks opsonization and complement fixation *Coagulase*- activates prothrombin *Hemolysin*- destroys RBCs, PMNs, M0s, platelets *Leukocidin*- destroys WBCs	*S. saprophyticus*: Novobiocin resistant

S. *epidermitis:* associated w/ IV catheters, damaged/prosthetic **heart valves: INSIDIOUS onset, Nosocomial, LESS virulent**. Blood culture Contaminant

S. *saprophyticus:* **Community acquired UTI** in young women

Streptococcus viridans (GABHS)

(non-motile, non-sporeforming) Gm+ cocci

Diseases	Characteristics	Habitat	Pathogenesis	Diagnosis
1	2	3	4	5
**Pharyngitis*- "strep throat", erythema, tonsillar exudate, fever **Skin/soft tissue* infections- impetigo,	Gm + cocci in chains or pairs Beta-hemolytic are classified by Lancefield groups	Human throat/ skin, Transmission by respiratory droplets	*Hyaluronidase*- degrades proteoglycans (TISSUE SPREAD) *Erythrogenic toxins* carlet fever,	All Strep are Catalase – Beta hemolysis and Bacitracin sensitivity point to GABHS, especially with inc. ASO titer

(Contd...)

1	2	3	4	5
cellulitis, necrotizing fasciitis **Scarlet fever-* centrifugal, red rash, erythrogenic toxin, slap cheek, strawberry tongue **Tox shock* syndrome- clinically like Staph TSS **Rheumatic fcver-* fever, myocarditis, polyarthritis, chorea, subcutaneous nodules, erythema marginatum rash. Mitral valve disease follows pharyngitis, NOT skin infections. Abs *vs.* bacteria cross react w/ joint and heart antigens **Acute GN-* hypertension, hematuria, edema of face/ ankles. Follows both pharyngitis AND skin infections. Cross reactive antigens deposited in GBM.	(A,B,D) according to C-carbo-hydrates		lysogenized S.pyogenes *Streptolysin 0-* results in beta hemolysis, target of ASO antibodies *M protein-* antibody target, but inhibits complement/ phagocytosis *Streptokinase-* converts plasminogen to plasmin, dissolves fibrin clots IgA protease	

S. agalactiae
(Group B strep)

Diseases	Characteristics	Habitat	Pathogenesis	Diagnosis
Neonatal menigitis, sepsis Pneumonia	*Beta-hemolytic*	Female urinary tract		

S. faecalis
(enterococcus)

Diseases	Characteristics	Habitat	Pathogenesis	Diagnosis
Subacute endocarditis, UTI	*Not hemolytic*	GI tract		Grows in 6.5% NaCl

S. bovis
(group D)

Diseases	Characteristics	Habitat	Pathogenesis	Diagnosis
UTI	Not hemolytic			Hydrolyze esculin in presence of bile. Not grow in 6.5% bile

S. pneumonia
(pneumococcus)

Diseases	Characteristics	Habitat	Pathogenesis	Diagnosis
Lobar pneumonia, Adult meningitis, URI (kids)	*Alpha-hemolytic*	Nasopharynx	85 different capsular polysaccarides	Quellung reaction

S. Mutans, mitis
(Viridans group)

Diseases	Characteristics	Habitat	Pathogenesis	Diagnosis
Subacute endocarditis, caries	*Alpha-hemolytic*	Oropharynx		

Neisseria

(Chocolate agar, Oxidase +, kidney bean shape) Gm-cocci

N. meningitides (meningococcus)

Diseases	Characteristics	Habitat	Pathogenesis	Diagnosis
**Meaningo-coccemia*-* fever, arthralgias, myalgias, petechial rash, inc. in people w/complement deficiencies *meaningitis-fever, headache, stiff neck, photophobia, inc. PMNs in CSF **Waterhouse-Friedrichsen*-* fever, purpura, DIC, adrenal insufficiency due to bilateral adrenal hemorrhage, shock, death (like a bad meningo-coccemia)	Gm-cocci kidney beans. Thayer-Martin, chocolate agar	Airborne droplets, colonized nasopharynx, establishes carrier states in some	Polysaccharide capsule, endotoxin (LPS), IgA protease Capsular polysaccharides are antigenic serve as markers for classification.	*Ferments maltose* Presumptive diagnosis by Gm stain of petechiae or CSF *Latex agglutination* test b/c capsular polysaccharides

N. gonnorhoeae (Gonococcus) (most common notifiable disease in US)

Diseases	Characteristics	Habitat	Pathogenesis	Diagnosis
1	2	3	4	5
Males—symptomatic dysuria, penile discharge b/c of urethritis.	No Capsule Gm-cocci kidney beans. Thayer-Martin, chocolate agar	Sexual transmission Often coexistent with Chlamydia and	Pili/fimbriae (Antigenic vriation) LPS OMPs IgA protease	*Men*: Gm-diplococci in PMNs Does not ferment

(Contd...)

1	2	3	4	5
Leads to epididymitis, prostatitis, urethral structures *Female*—asymptomatic, vaginal discharge, dyspareunia,due to cervicitis, Infertility, PID, ectopic, tubo-ovarian abcess, perihepatitis (Fitz-Hugh-Curtis syndrome), opthalmia neonatorum Both: Septic arthritis		Syphillis (tx w/ tetracyclineor chloramphenacol)	No Capsule!	maltose No serologic testing, no capsule!

Clostridium

(Anaerobic, spore-forming, with Exotoxin) Gm + Rods

C. tetani

Diseases	Characteristics	Habitat	Pathogenesis	Diagnosis
Tetanus—tetany, risus sardonicus 'joker smile', exaggerated reflexes, respiratory failure		Spores, ubiquitous in soil, enter wounds and germinate in anaerobic environment of necrotic tissue	Tetanus toxin travels intra axonally to CNS, blocks release of inhibitory glycine Neurotrans-mitter	

C. botulinum

Diseases	Characteristics	Habitat	Pathogenesis	Diagnosis
1	2	3	4	5
Botulism "flaccid paralysis",		Spores, in soil, inadequate sterlization of	Botulinum toxin ingested preformed. Tox	

(Contd...)

1	2	3	4	5
descending weakness, diplopia, flaccid paralysis, resp failure. *Wound botulism*—spores to wounds, germinate, release toxin *Infant botulism*—ingestion ofspores in honey-floppy baby		canned foods. Alkaline veggies, smoked fish.	spreads in blood, to nerves blocks Ach Release Toxin can be used to Tx torticollis, blepharospasm	

C. perfingens

Diseases	Characteristics	Habitat	Pathogenesis	Diagnosis
Gas gangrene (myonecrosis): war wounds, septic abortions *Food poisoning*-ingestion of cooking resistant spores in foods. Watery diarrhoea, cramps, little vomiting	Results in crepitus-gas production and Hemolysis	Normal flora of colon and vagina	Alpha tox-lecithinase degrades cell membranesh-emolytic	Morphylogy, exudate smears, culture, sugar fermentation, organic acid production

C. difficile

Diseases	Characteristics	Habitat	Pathogenesis	Diagnosis
Antibiotic associated pseudomem-branous colitis-esp in	Normal flora in 3% of People	Suppression of normal flora allows overgrowth, usually by clindamycin,	ID C-diff tox in stool	

(Contd...)

1	2	3	4	5
hospitalized pts.		ampicillin, cephalosporins Exotox A (severe diarrhoea) Exotox B (damage to colonic mucosa)		

Bacillus

(Anaerobic, spore-forming, with Exotoxin) Gm + Rods

B. anthracis

Diseases	Characteristics	Habitat	Pathogenesis	Diagnosis
Woolsorter's disease pulmonary anthrax, pneumonia	Large w/ square ends, non-motile	Common in animals. Human infected by spores on animal products (skins/hides) Transmission through skin, GI tract, respiratory tract	Antiphagocytic capsule made of d-glutamate [only one w/ Amino acids!] (not a polysaccharide) Tripartite anthrax toxin: protective antigen, lethal factor, edema factor. Protective factors inhibits phagocytosis	Morphology and blood agar growth.

B. cereus

Diseases	Characteristics	Habitat	Pathogenesis	Diagnosis
Vomiting with 4 hr incubation period (like S. aureus)-*heat stable toxin—*	Distinguished from B. anthracis by motility and lack of capsule.	Sporeson grains survive cooking and germinate when food is warmed.	*Preformed heat-labile exterotoxin* (like E. coli, Cholera tox)-diarrhoea	

Corynebacterium diptheriae
(non-motile, non-sporeforming, Chinese) Gm + Rods

Diseases	Characteristics	Habitat	Pathogenesis	Diagnosis
Diptheria—throat inflammation, gray fibrinous exudate (pseudo-membrane), airway obstruction, myocarditis, recurrent laryngeal nerve palsy	Club shaped, in palisades, Chinese characters Polyphosphate granules stain metachro-matically	Airborne droplets, colonization of throat and production of Diptheria tox.	Diptheria tox: inhibits protein syn by ADP ribosylation of eukaryotic ef-2. Toxin produced by lysogenized bacteria (like erythrogenic toxin of GABHS)	Tellurite plate, Loefller's Toxin assessed by animal inoculation or gel diffusion precipitin test.

Listeria monocytogenes
(Facultative intracellular anerobes, Non-sporeforming, tumbling motility) Gm + Rods

Diseases	Characteristics	Habitat	Pathogenesis	Diagnosis
Neonatal meningitis and sepsis, abortion, premature delivery	Gm + rods, in clumps, Chinese characters, NON-sporeforming, Tumbling distinguishes it from Corynebacterium	Newborns, immunocom-promised are high risk groups. Transmitted to humans from animal feces, veggies, unpasteurized milk/cheese.	Only Gm+ with LPS Infects monocytes and induces granulomas. Listeriolysin O punches holes in cells	Gm+ rods, beta hemolysis, motility

Enteric Gram Negative Rods

Note: Not all gram negative enterics belong to *Enterobacteriaciae family: 1) colonic location 2) facultative anaerobes 3)ferment glucose, 4)oxidase negative, and 5)reduce nitrates to nitrites. ALL are members here except:* Vibrio, Campylobacter, Helicobacter, Pseudomonas, Bacteriodes. ("Vile People Can't Be Happy") As a group, *Enterobacteriaciae* are often normal flora. Pathogenisis is by endotoxin/ LPS, exotoxins. O (Outer polysaccharides), H (flagHella), K (Kapsular polysaccharides) are important antigens. Inoculation on MacConkey's or Eosin-Methylene Blue (EMB) agar differentiates family members by lactose fermenting ability. Fermenters are pink-purple, non-fermenters are colourless. Also keep an eye on motility.

Enteric *(Intestinal and non-Intestinal disease) Gm-Rods*

E. coli (Enterobacteriaciae)

Diseases	Characteristics	Habitat	Pathogenesis	Diagnosis
Most common UTI, Gm-sepsis, traveller's diarrhoea. 2nd most common cause of Neonatal meningitis. *Enterotoxigenic strains:* Do NOT invade! heat labile enterotox binds GM1 ganglioside receptor, activates adenylate cyclase via ADPribosylation of G protein. (like Cholera tox) Watery diarrhoea. *Enterohemorragic:* verotoxin inhibits 60s ribosome (like Shigella) Bloody diarrhoea. 0157:H7 type causes hemolytic-uremic syndrome (anaemia, thrombocy-topenia, renal failure) associated w/ fast food outbreaks *Enteroinvasive*: factor mediated invasion of epithelial cells, sepsis. Bloody diarrhoea with WBCs.	As other enterobacteria ciae family	Normal flora, but need Virulence factors to cause disease.	Pathogenisis by pilus and enterotox, capsule, and endotoxin. Serotype ID by O,H,K antigens	Ferments lactose, unlike Salmonella, Shigella

Salmonella (Enerobacteriaciae)

Diseases	Characteristics	Habitat	Pathogenesis	Diagnosis
S. enteritidis causes gasteroenteritis via Cholera like tox. Large inoculum needed. (Peptic acid kills) Tx symptoms. S.typhi -Typhoid fever, init by asymptomatic infection of gut phagocytes and dissemination to liver, Gall bladder (carrier state), Fever, RLQ abdominal pain, rose spots. Tx Cipro or ceftriaxone. S. cholerae-suis- Gm- sepsis. Esp patients with Sickle cell (risk for osteomyelitis b/c func. Asplenia)	As other enterobacteria-ciae family	Normal flora of animals. Contamination food, poultry / eggs	K anitgen/Vi antigen Flagella antigenic variation	Does NOT ferment lactose. Production of H_2S gas distinguish from Shigella.

ENTERIC *(Intestial disease) Gm-Rods*

Shigella (Enterobacteriaciae)

Diseases	Characteristics	Habitat	Pathogenesis	Diagnosis
Enterocolitis (dysentary) by S.dysentariae, S.sonnei, S. flexneri, S. boydii	Non-motile Small innoculum <100 bugs	Not normal flora. Humans only host. 4Fs: fingers flied food feces (fecaloral)	Distal ileal and colonic mucosal invasion and cell death. Does NOT enter bloodstream (unlike Salmonella)	NO H_2S gas, non-motile. Non lactose fermenting on EMB, MacConkey's agar PMNs in smear w/ fever suggest invasive bug

Vibrio (*Not Enterobacteriaciae*)

Diseases	Characteristics	Habitat	Pathogenesis	Diagnosis
Cholera - Massive watery diarrhoea (Rice water stool) like enterotoxic E.coli V.parahemo-lyticus is a marine bug in contaminated raw seafood. Japan	Comma shaped, single flagella. Large innoculum needed.	Infects humans only, transmission by fecaloral.	Mucinase aided colonization of small intestine, bipartite enterotox: binds GM1 gangliosides on enterocyte, ADPribosylation of G protein. (like ETEC)	Diagnosis clinically in endemic areas: Asia, Africa, Latin America.

Campylobacter (*Not Enterobacteriaciae*)

Diseases	Characteristics	Habitat	Pathogenesis	Diagnosis
More frequently causes enterocolitis than Salmonella or Shigella. Can cause bloody diarrhoea	Comma or Sshaped, Microaerophilic, urease negative	Domestic animals via fecal oral, unpasteurized milk	Probably enterotoxin	Blood agar w/ antibiotics, C.jejuni grows at 42C, produces oxidase, nalidixix acid sensitive C.intestinalis grows at 25C, oxidase neg, resistant to nalidixic acid

Helicobacter *pylori* (*Not Enterobacteriaciae*)

Diseases	Characteristics	Habitat	Pathogenesis	Diagnosis
Gastritis, peptic ulcer, risk factor Gastric carcinoma	Urease + (protects from stomach acid)	Fecal-oral.	Attaches to gastric mucosa, mediated by NH_3 production, host inflammatory response	

ENTERIC *(EXTRAINTESTIAL disease)* Gm-Rods

Klebsiella-Enterofacter-Serratia (*Enterobacteriaciae*)

Diseases	Characteristics	Habitat	Pathogenesis	Diagnosis
Opportunistic pathogens cause UTI, pneumonia, usually nosocomial Klebsiella is non-motile, with capsule, mucoid colony appearance. Klebsiella pneumo renowned for severity, bloody 'currant jelly' sputum, lung cavitations. Serratia-bright red pigment. Nosocomial-Ab resistant	All ferment Lactose K.pneumoniae, E.cloacae, S.marcescens difficult to Distinguish Clinically	Large intestine, soil water		Ferment lactose on EMB, MacConkey's agar

Proteus-Providencia-Morganella (*Enterobacteriaciae*)

Diseases	Characteristics	Habitat	Pathogenesis	Diagnosis
Community and nosocomial UTI, c high motility Important species: Proteus mirabilis, Proteus vularis Providencia stgretii morganii)	Non lactose fermenting, urease + (alkalinizes urine) Only enterobac that makes Phenylalanine Deaminase	Large intestine, soil water		Swarming appearance on blood agar. Use antigens from Rickettsiae cross react with Proteus. P.mirabilis is indole neg unlike others of this group.

Pseudomonas (*Not Enterobacteriaciae*)

Diseases	Characteristics	Habitat	Pathogenesis	Diagnosis
P aeruginosa: opportunistic, *nosocomial:* Pneumonia, osteomyelitis, burn infections, sepsis, UTI, endocarditis, malignant otitis externa, corneal infections. P. cepacia colonizes CF patients	Strict aerobe, Not glucose fermenting, Not reduce nitrates, oxidase +	Normal flora of colon.	Exotox like C.diptheriae (ADPreibo-sylation)	Produces pyocyanin, pyoverdin

Bacteroides fragilis (*Not Enterobacteriaciae*)

Diseases	Characteristics	Habitat	Pathogenesis	Diagnosis
Peritoneal abscesses. Growth favoured by growth w/ facultative anaerobes to exhause local oxygen	Anaerobic, non sporeforming, non LPS, polysaccharide capsule. No exotox, No LPS	Predominant flora of colon. NOT communicable. Exits colon via break in mucosa (Chronic disease, PID, trauma)	Polysaccharide capsule provides virulence factor	

RESPIRATORY *Gm-Rods*

H. Influenzae (*chocolate agar w/heme and NAD*)

Diseases	Characteristics	Habitat	Pathogenesis	Diagnosis
Leading cause of meningitis in kids. Peak at 6m to 1 yr. (decline in maternal IgG, inability of infants to mount attack *vs.* polysaccharide capsule) Fatal epiglottitis by type B influenzae.	Coccobacillus w/ polysaccharide Capsule	Upper respiratory tract, respiratory droplets	ONLY encapsulated forms like type B cause invasive disease. Non-encapsu-lated cause URI, pneumonia in pts with preexisting lung disease (COPD). IgA protease,	Chocolate agar, w/ heme and NAD. Quellung rxn

Legionella pneumophilia (Cysteine and Iron agar)

Diseases	Characteristics	Habitat	Pathogenesis	Diagnosis
Atypical pneumonia with high fever, non-productive cough (differentiate from Mycoplasma, influenza, psittacosis, Q fever)	Poor gm stain	Airborne from water Sources. Smoking EtOH, Immuno suppressed are at risk.		High concentration Error! No table of figures entries found.of cysteine and iron. Urine antigen test. Suspect when inc. PMNs with no organisms!

Bordetella pertussis (*Bordet-genou agar*)

Diseases	Characteristics	Habitat	Pathogenesis	Diagnosis
Whooping cough- acute tracheobronchitis with URI symptoms, paroxysmal hacking cough 1-4 wks, copious mucus	Small gm- rods	Airborn droplets (highly contagious)	Polysaccharide capsule and pili are essential for virulence. Does NOT invade. Pertussis tox (ADP-ribosylation), and tracheal cytotoxin.	Culture on Bordetgenou agar. Ab agglutination, stain

ZOONTIC *Gm-Rods*

Brucella (*virulent, facultative intracellular, tx: aminoglycoside*)

Diseases	Characteristics	Habitat	Pathogenesis	Diagnosis
Brucellosis- influenza like syndrome w/ undulating fever(higher during day, lower at night). Lymphade-nopathy, H/Smegaly, no boboes/ulcers.	Small gm- rods	Animal reserviors: B melitensisi (goats/sheep) B. abortus (cattle) B. suis (pigs) Non-pasteurized milk products (travellers), through skin (meat packers, vets, farmers)	Organisms localize in RES. Persist in macrophages, induce granulomas	Serology, biochemistry

Francisella tularensis (*virulent, facultative intracellular, tx: aminoglycoside*)

Diseases	Characteristics	Habitat	Pathogenesis	Diagnosis
Tularemia- influenza like syndrome w/ ulceroglandular lesions (hole in skin, black base, swollen LN, draining pus)	Small gm- rods	Ubiquitous in US in wide variety of animals. Tick/mite vectors. Humans as accidental dead end hosts by bites or animal skin handling.	Enters through skin, localizes in RES. Persist in macrophages, induce granulomas	Serology

Yersinia pestis (*virulent, facultative intracellular, tx: aminoglycoside*)

Diseases	Characteristics	Habitat	Pathogenesis	Diagnosis
Plague- Hematogenous spread results in fever myalgias, hemorrhage. Also septic shock, pneumonia.	Small gm- rods with bipolar stain	Endemic in prairie dogs in US, 99% cases in SE Asia. Rats/flease in urban centers. Also woundperson Respiratory droplets.	Bacteria spread to regional LN, enlarged tender buboes.	Immuno florescence

Pasteurella multocida

Diseases	Characteristics	Habitat	Pathogenesis	Diagnosis
Cellulitis rapid onset at bite site. Osteomyelitis as complication. Sutures predispose to infection	Small gm- rods	Normal flora of dogs and cats. Transmitted to humans by animal bite.		Presumptive Dx by rapid onset cellulitis at animal bite.

MYCOBACTERIA
(Obligate aerobe, faculative intracellular organisms)
Acid Fast Rods

M. tuberculosis

Diseases	Characteristics	Habitat	Pathogenesis	Diagnosis
Tuberculosis: chronic low grade fever, night sweats, productive cough, hemoptysis, weight loss. Elderly, immunocomp, malnourished at risk.	Obligate aerobe, intracellular, infect M0, persist for years. Mycolic acid walls	Only infects humans. Respiratory aerosol. Infects M0s in mid/lower lobes, init granuloma formation, widely disseminate the infection. T cells help M0 kill some intracellular mycobacteria at expense of bystander cell damage. Result: necrotic host cells, viable mycobacteria. Walled off w/ giant cells, fibroblasts, collagen, calcification to form granuloma or tubercle. This 1' infection = Ghon focus on CXR (when including Ca tubercles in perihilar lymph nodes = Ghon complex.) Reactivation prefers upper lobe (obligate aerobe) of lung. Reactivation can infect any organ. Cervical LN (scrofula),spine (Pott's disease.)	Mycolic acids confer acid fastness. WaxD is active ingredient in Freund's adjuvant. Cord factor is virulence factor (mycoside= 2 mycolic acids + disaccharide)	PPD tests for prior exposure or to BCG vax. Positive test if both redness, induration 48-72 hr after injection (DTH rxn.) *Note*: candida and mumps as controls in immunocomp. Acid fast stain. NaOH concentrate on Lowenstein-Jensen medium. Slow culture, 6-8 wks. Niacin production

M. avium-intracellulare

Diseases	Characteristics	Habitat	Pathogenesis	Diagnosis
Clincal TB indistinguishable from M tuberculosis in AIDS.	Atypical mycobacterium	Found in water, soil, not pathogenic in guinea pigs (infects birds)		

M. leprae

Diseases	Characteristics	Habitat	Pathogenesis	Diagnosis
Leprosy- preferential growth in < 37C, skin, superficial nerves. Tuberculoid- good cellular immune response, few AFB, granulomas, positive lepromin skin test. Anethetized skin lesions and thickened superficial nerves. Lepromatous- poor cellular immune response, lots of organisms, foamy histiocytes, negative lepromin skin test (poor response.) Skin lesions, lion facies. Skin anesthesia, bone resorption, skin thickening, disfiguring.	Never has Been grown in lab.	Brazil, India, Sudan Humans only natural hosts. Mouse footpad and armadillo growth only. Transmission by nasal secretions, skin lesions to persons with prolonged contact with patients.	Intracellular replication (skin histiocytes, endothelial cells, Schwann cells)	

ACTINOMYCETES *(Gm-Branching Rods)*

A. Israelii

Diseases	Characteristics	Habitat	Pathogenesis	Diagnosis
Actinomycosis- hard non-tender swelling, drains pus through sinus. (abscess that spreads to neck, chest, abdomen.)	Anaerobic Gmbranching rods	Normal anaerobic flora oral cavity/GI tract. Not communicable.	Invasion after local trauma (risk factor for anaerobic growth)	Anaerobic Gmbranching rods, sulfur granules in pus

Nocardia asteroids (Acid Fast Branching)

Diseases	Characteristics	Habitat	Pathogenesis	Diagnosis
Nocardiosis- pneumonia that progresses to abscess formation, sinus tract drainage, dissemination to brain/kidney (immuno-suppressed)	Aerobic Gmbranching rods.	Soil, NOT normal flora		Acid fast branching, NO sulfur, aerobic

Mycoplasma pneumonia *(No cell wall, poor gm stain) Small free living organism)*

Diseases	Characteristics	Habitat	Pathogenesis	Diagnosis
"Walking pneumonia" (dry non-productive cough, horrible CST, generally feel well) Most common pneumonia in young adults (college students).	Smallest free living organism, no cell wall so poor gm stain, resists penicillins, cephalosporins. Cell membrane has chol which are not in other bacteria. 'Fried egg' colonies on Eaton's agar. ('Eat Fried Eggs with cholesterol')	Respiratory droplets. Attaches but does NOT invade respiratory epithelium, like B.pertussis.	Pathogenic only for humans. Arrests cilliary motion, induces epithelial cell necrosis. Cross reactive antigens induce anti RBC autoantibodies (cold agglutinins.)	Elevated titer of cold agglutinins or specific anitbodies

CHAPTER

15

Bacterial Diagnostic Chart

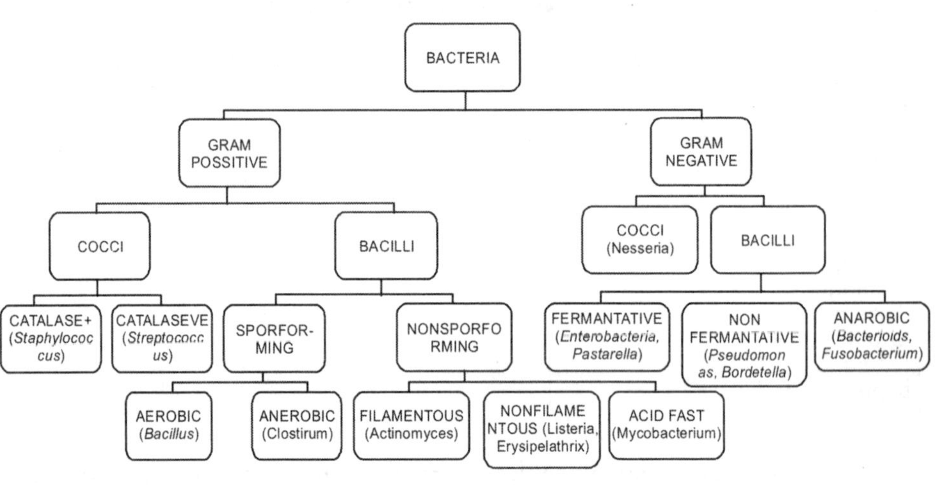

Organism	gram rx.	cellular shape & arrange-ment	glucose fermen-tation*	lactose fermen-tation*	nitrate reduc-tion to nitrite	nitrate reduc-tion to N_2	motility	indole produc-tion	starch hydro-lysis	catalase rx.
1	2	3	4	5	6	7	8	9	10	11
Escherichia Coli	–	short rods	FG	FG	+	–	+	+	–	+
Klebsiella pneumoniae	–	short rods	FG	FG	+	–	–	–	–	+
Serratia marcescens	–	short rods	FG or F	(F) or –	+	–	+	–	–	+
Pseudomonas fluorescens	–	rods	–	–	–	+	+ or –	–	–	+

(Contd...)

1	2	3	4	5	6	7	8	9	10	11
Chromobacterium violaceum	–	rods	F	–	+	–	+	–	–	+
Micrococcus Luteus	+	cocci in clusters	–	–	–	–	–	–	–	+
Staphylococcus epidermidis	+	cocci in clusters	F	F	+	–	–	–	–	+
Enterococcus Faecalis	+	cocci in chains	F	F	(+) or –	–	–	–	–	–
Lactobacillus plantarum	+	rods	F	F	(+) or –	–	–	–	–	–
Bacillus Subtilis	+	rods	–	–	+	–	+ or –	–	+	+
Bacillus Cereus	+	large rods	F	–	+	–	+ or –	–	+	+
Bacillus Polymyxa	+	rods	FG	FG	+	–	+ or –	–	+	+
Bacillus *megaterium***	+	large rods	–	–	–	–	+ or –	–	+	+

rx—reaction

FG—fermentation with gas

FG—fermentation without gas

+—positive

-—negative

*—for glucose &lactose fermentation broth

CHAPTER 16

List of Bioinformatics Software

Sequence Analysis Software

1. Base calling, assembling, viewing: Phred / Phrap / Consed
2. SNP Analysis: Consed, DnaSP, PolyPhred, SNPidentifier, SNP PHAGE, SNPdetector, Consed
3. Alignment / Clustering: Arachne, Assembler, CAP3, ClustalW, ContigViewer, ePCR, mePCR, MultiAlin, PaCE, PCAP, Splign, Alignment Graphic Drawing | SSAHA, MAQ, Bowtie, Mosaic
4. Check low complexity: RepeatMasker, Repeatfinder
5. RNAi searches: miRanda, MiRFinder, others
6. Similarity Search: Blast, Blastz, Fasta, GMAP, Mulan, SynView, SynBrowse, ECR Browser, Others
7. Primer design: Amplify, CodeHOP, Expeditor, OligoSpawn, FastPCR, Primer3, Primer Premier 5, Prim2
8. Next Gen Seq Analysis: A list of next-gen-seq software
9. Genome Analysis: Light weighted genome viewer, Vmatch
10. Misc.: Reverse complement convertor, KegDraw

Genetics Analysis Software

1. Linkage analysis: CarthaGene, Cri-Map, JoinMap, LocusMAP, Mapmaker, NCBI CONCORDE, RHMapper, Sibs, Locusmap, SCAT, HOTSPOTTER
2. Haplotype analysis: fastPHASE, PHASE
3. Genetics analysis: epiSNP, EPISNPmpi, MiNiInbred

4. QTL analysis: BmapQTL, MapQTL, QTL Cartographer, QTL Express, QTLBIM, Qxpak, PlabQTL, SPSSQTL, WebQTL, more ...
5. Phylogeny analysis: Phylip, PAUP, PhyML, TimeTree, Eshadow, Others
6. Pedigree: Pedigraph, Pedigree-Draw, MiniInbred, MORGAN (Monte Carlo Genetic Analysis, includes pedcheck, genedrop, etc.)

Functional Genomics Software

1. Domain/Motif Prediction: EST Scan, ORF Finder, ORFpredictor, Genome Scan, Pfam, PRINTS, PROSITE, Splice Predictor, more ...
2. Gene Prediction: Augusrus, HMMgene, GENEscan, Grail, GLEAN, Jigsaw
3. Microarray Analysis: ArrayGenes, KegArray, HDB Stat, Power Atlas, more...
4. Genome analysis: GenomatiX, PepTool, Genewiz, Others (GeneScan, Genie, HMMGene).
5. Gene Annotation and Analysis: Apollo, AmiGO, ENSMART, GoSurfer, GeneHopper, KegHier, CateGOrizer, GeneLynx, MatchMiner, Ontology On-line, Otterlace, Resourcerer, Visual Annotation Display
6. Expressoin data analysis: DAVID and EASE, GenMAPP, Gaggle, Spotfire, TM4
7. Comparative analysis: COGs, PEDANT 3, KEGG, TheSEED, GenDB, PUMA2

Genetic Networks and System Biology

1. Ontology: OBO Edit, COB Edit, Phenote, Protege Editor, Semantic Web
2. Trait/phenotype analysis: TASSEL (for Association Mapping)
3. Software suites: SynBioSS, ToppGene Suite, GATACA, System Biology.ORG, Systems-Biology.ORG

General Applications

1. Databases: AceDB, MySQL, PostgreSQL, Entrez Programming Utilities, perl DBI, PHP
2. LIMS: Pipeline pilot, Progeny, more ...
3. Packages: EMBOSS (contains over 150 applications), GMOD (CMap, FlashGViewer, GBrowse, PubSearch, TextPresso) BioMOBY, BioRuby, NCBI Tool Kit, Biology WorkBench (SDSC)

4. Programming Tools: BioPerl, BioJava, R
5. Programmable Database Access: EUtilities (NCBI), Ensembl Perl API

Links to software resources

1. Canadian Bioinformatics Help Desk Software Repository
2. NRSP-8 Animal Genomics Software Repository
3. INRA Software Repository
4. NIH Molecular Biology Software List
5. ExPASy Proteomics Tools

Protein related databases

1. UniProt—the universal protein resource (including UniProtKB -Swiss-Prot and TrEMBL-, UniRef, UniParc)
2. Around UniProtKB—links to related databases and portals
3. HAMAP—Portal to microbial UniProtKB/Swiss-Prot entries
4. SwissVar—Portal to human diseases and variant information in UniProtKB/Swiss-Prot
5. UniPathway—Metabolic pathways database
6. ViralZone—Portal to viral UniProtKB/Swiss-Prot entries
7. HPI—Human Proteomics Initiative
8. PPAP—Plant Proteome Annotation Project
9. Tox-Prot—Toxin Annotation Project
10. neXtProt—A knowledge platform dedicated to human proteins
11. Swiss Human Plasma protein dataset—Novartis/Geneprot MicroProt2 dataset from Human Plasma samples
12. NCBI protein resources
13. InterPro—Integrated Resources of Proteins Domains and Functional Sites
14. PROSITE—Database of protein families and domains
15. BLOCKS—BLOCKS db
16. Gene3D—Structural and Functional Annotation of Protein Families
17. Panther—Functional classification system
18. Pfam—Protein families db (HMM derived) [Mirrors at JFRC (USA), CCBB (South Korea) Institute, UK, Karolinska Institutet (Sweden)]
19. PIRSF—Protein classification system

20. PRINTS—Protein Motif fingerprint db
21. ProDom—Protein domain db (Automatically generated)
22. SBASE—SBASE domain db
23. SMART—Simple Modular Architecture Research Tool
24. SUPERFAMILY—Library of profile HMMs representing all proteins of known structure
25. STRING—Search Tool for the Retrieval of Interacting Genes/Proteins
26. TIGRFAMs—TIGR protein families db
27. BIND—Biomolecular Interaction Network Database
28. DIP—Database of Interacting Proteins
29. MINT—Molecular Interaction database
30. HPRD—Human Protein Reference Database
31. IntAct
32. BioGRID—General Repository for Interaction Dataset
33. PPI—JCB Protein-Protein Interaction Website
34. PMD—Protein Mutant db

Protein 3D structure related databases

(*a*) PDB—Protein Data Bank

(*b*) PDBTM—Protein Data Bank of Transmembrane Proteins

(*c*) BioMagResBank—Repository for data on proteins, peptides, and nucleic acids from NMR spectroscopy

(*d*) SWISS-MODEL Repository—Automatically generated protein models db

(e) ModBase—Db of comparative protein structure models

(*f*) CATH—UCL BSM structural classification of proteins

(*g*) SCOP —Structural classification of proteins [Mirrors]

(*h*) HCA—Hydrophobic Cluster Database

(*i*) Molecules To Co —Molecules To Go (formerly known as Molecules R Us), browser for PDB

(*j*) BMM Domain Fishing—Biomolecular Modelling Laboratory (ICRF) protein domain fishing

(*k*) Relibase—Receptor/ligand complexes db [Mirror in USA]

(*l*) CCDC—Cambridge Crystallographic Data Center (Cambridge Stuctural Db (CSD))

(*m*) HSSP—Homology-derived secondary structure of proteins db

(*n*) MutaProt—Comparison of PDB files which differ by point mutations

(*o*) DisProt—Database of Protein Disorder

(*p*) SWISS-3DIMAGE—3D images of proteins and other biological macromolecules

PROTEOMICS DATABASES AND LINKS

Gel-based data

(*a*) MIAPEGelDB—A public repository for MIAPE Gel electrophoresis documents

(*b*) WORLD-2DPAGE List—Links to known 2-D PAGE database servers, as well as to 2-D PAGE related servers and services

(*c*) World-2DPAGE Repository—A public standards-compliant repository for gel-based proteomics data published in the literature

(*d*) The World-2DPAGE Constellation—Promote and publish gel-based proteomics data through the ExPASy server

(*e*) Proteomics Links page of the Swiss Proteomics Society

Mass spectrometry data

(*a*) GPMdb—Global Proteome Machine Database

(*b*) OPD—Open Proteomics Database (currently down)

(*c*) PeptideAtlas—peptides identified in tandem mass spectrometry proteomics experiments

(*d*) PRIDE—PRoteomics IDEntifications database

(*e*) Tranche—Peer-to-peer distributed file system

Nucleotide and related databases

(*a*) EMBL—EMBL Nucleotide sequence db (EBI)

(*b*) Genbank—GenBank Nucleotide Sequence db (NCBI)

(*c*) DDBJ—DNA Data Bank of Japan

(*d*) dbEST—dbEST (Expressed Sequence Tags) db (NCBI)

(*e*) dbSTS—dbSTS (Sequence Tagged Sites) db (NCBI)

(*f*) Ensembl—Genome database for vertebrates and other eukaryotic species

(*g*) UCSC Genome Browser

(*h*) AsDb—Aberrant Splicing db

(*i*) ACUTS—Ancient conserved untranslated DNA sequences db

(*j*) Codon Usage Db

(*k*) EPD—Eukaryotic Promoter db

(*l*) HOVERGEN—Homologous Vertebrate Genes db

(*m*) IMGT—ImMunoGeneTics db [Mirror at EBI]

(*n*) RDP—Ribosomal db Project

(*o*) PLACE—Plant cis-acting regulatory DNA elements db

(*p*) PlantCARE—Plant cis-acting regulatory DNA elements db

(*q*) smiRNAdb—Information about mammalian small RNAs

(*r*) ssu rRNA—Small ribosomal subunit at the European ribosomal RNA database

(*s*) lsu rRNA—Large ribosomal subunit at the European ribosomal RNA database

(*t*) 5S rRNA—5S ribosomal RNA db

(*u*) greengenes—16S rRNA gene database and workbench

(*v*) tmRNA Website

(*w*) tmRDB—tmRNA dB

(*x*) tRNA—tRNA compilation from the University of Bayreuth

(*y*) RNA editing—RNA editing site

(*z*) RNAmod db—RNA modification db

(*aa*) MPDB—Molecular probe db

(*bb*) VectorDB—Vector sequence db

Carbohydrates resources

(*a*) FCCA—Forum Carbohydrates Coming of Age

(*b*) GlycoSuiteDB—Db of glycan structures

(*c*) Monosacharide browser—Space filling Fischer projection for monosaccharides

(*d*) genomics resource for animal lectins

SPECIES SPECIFIC DATABASES

Human

(1) OMIM—Online Mendelian Inheritance in Man

(2) GENATLAS—Human genes atlas

(3) GeneTests—Medical genetics knowledge base
(4) GeneCards—Db integrating information on human genes
(5) GeneLoc—Integrated map of the human genome (ex- UDB)
(6) Ensembl Human genome browser
(7) The Gene Index Project—ex-TIGR Human Gene Indices
(8) Hs UniGene—Human transcripts in GenBank (EST clusters)
(9) STACK—Sequence Tag Alignment and Consensus Knowledgebase (Db of consensus human ESTs)
(10) Allgenes.org—Human predicted gene index/catalog
(11) GeneLynx—Portal to the human genome
(12) HUGE—Human Unidentified Gene-Encoded large proteins cDNA (KIAA...)
(13) CGAP—Cancer Genome Anatomy Project
(14) MGC—Mammalian Gene Collection
(15) SCDb—Stem cell db
(16) Homophila—Human Disease to Drosophila gene db
(17) Human Protein Atlas—Displays the expression and localization of proteins in a large variety of normal human tissues and cancer cells
(18) Progenetix CGH database—Molecular Cytogenetics in Leukaemia and Cancer
(19) Contribution of the Sanger Centre to chromosomes 1,6,9,10,11,13,20,22 and X
(20) Chr1 UniProtKB/Swiss-Prot—entries, gene names and cross-references to MIM
(21) Chr2 UniProtKB/Swiss-Prot—entries, gene names and cross-references to MIM
(22) Chr3 UniProtKB/Swiss-Prot—entries, gene names and cross-references to MIM
(23) Chr4 UniProtKB/Swiss-Prot—entries, gene names and cross-references to MIM
(24) Chr5 UniProtKB/Swiss-Prot—entries, gene names and cross-references to MIM
(25) Chr6 UniProtKB/Swiss-Prot—entries, gene names and cross-references to MIM
(26) Chr7 UniProtKB/Swiss-Prot—entries, gene names and cross-references to MIM

(27) Chr8 UniProtKB/Swiss-Prot—entries, gene names and cross-references to MIM

(28) Chr9 UniProtKB/Swiss-Prot—entries, gene names and cross-references to MIM

(29) Chr10 UniProtKB/Swiss-Prot—entries, gene names and cross-references to MIM

(30) Chr11 UniProtKB/Swiss-Prot—entries, gene names and cross-references to MIM

(31) Chr12 UniProtKB/Swiss-Prot—entries, gene names and cross-references to MIM

(32) Chr13 UniProtKB/Swiss-Prot—entries, gene names and cross-references to MIM

(33) Chr14 UniProtKB/Swiss-Prot—entries, gene names and cross-references to MIM

(34) Chr15 UniProtKB/Swiss-Prot—entries, gene names and cross-references to MIM

(35) Chr16 UniProtKB/Swiss-Prot—entries, gene names and cross-references to MIM

(36) Chr17 UniProtKB/Swiss-Prot—entries, gene names and cross-references to MIM

(37) Chr18 UniProtKB/Swiss-Prot—entries, gene names and cross-references to MIM

(38) Chr19 UniProtKB/Swiss-Prot—entries, gene names and cross-references to MIM

(39) Chr20 UniProtKB/Swiss-Prot—entries, gene names and cross-references to MIM

(40) Chr21 UniProtKB/Swiss-Prot—entries, gene names and cross-references to MIM

(41) Chr22 at HGC—Human genome center for chromosome 22

(42) Chr22 UniProtKB/Swiss-Prot—entries, gene names and cross-references to MIM

(43) ChrX UniProtKB/Swiss-Prot—entries, gene names and cross-references to MIM

(44) ChrY UniProtKB/Swiss-Prot—entries, gene names and cross-references to MIM

(45) H-InvDB Database—Human gene db, with cDNA clones available from six high throughput cDNA sequencing projects

(46) Human Chromosome1 Launchpad
(47) Human Chromosome2 Launchpad
(48) Human Chromosome3 Launchpad
(49) Human Chromosome4 Launchpad
(50) Human Chromosome5 Launchpad
(51) Human Chromosome6 Launchpad
(52) Human Chromosome7 Launchpad
(53) Human Chromosome8 Launchpad
(54) Human Chromosome9 Launchpad
(55) Human Chromosome10 Launchpad
(56) Human Chromosome11 Launchpad
(57) Human Chromosome12 Launchpad
(58) Human Chromosome13 Launchpad
(59) Human Chromosome14 Launchpad
(60) Human Chromosome15 Launchpad
(61) Human Chromosome16 Launchpad
(62) Human Chromosome17 Launchpad
(63) Human Chromosome18 Launchpad
(64) Human Chromosome19 Launchpad
(65) Human Chromosome20 Launchpad
(66) Human Chromosome21 Launchpad
(67) Human Chromosome22 Launchpad
(68) Human ChromosomeX Launchpad
(69) Human ChromosomeY Launchpad

Vertebrates

(*a*) OMIA—Online Mendelian Inheritance in Animals
(*b*) MGI—Mouse Genome Informatics (includes MGD)
(*c*) Ensembl Mouse genome browser
(*d*) DFCI MGI—TIGR Mouse Gene Index
(*e*) Mm UniGene—Mouse transcripts in GenBank (EST clusters)
(*f*) MGC—Mammalian Gene Collection
(*g*) Mouse gene knockouts db
(*h*) RGD—Rat genome db
(*i*) Ensembl Rat genome browser

(*j*) RatMAP—Rat genome db
(*k*) DFCI RGI—TIGR Rat Gene Index
(*l*) Rn Unigene—Rat transcripts in GenBank (EST clusters)
(*m*) Ensembl Chimpanzee genome browser
(*n*) Ensembl Gorilla genome browser
(*o*) Ensembl Cat genome browser
(*p*) Ensembl Bovine genome browser
(*q*) Ensembl Dog genome browser
(*r*) Ensembl Horse genome browser
(*s*) Ensembl Pig genome browser
(*t*) Ensembl Rabbit genome browser
(*u*) BOVMAP—Bovine genome db (in France)
(*v*) NHGRI Dog Genome Project
(*w*) ArkDB—Cat, Chicken, Cow, Deer, Horse, Pig, Quail, Sheep, Turkey genome databases
(*x*) Ensembl Chicken genome browser
(*y*) FishBase—Global information system on fishes
(*z*) Fugu genome project
(*aa*) Fugu—HGMP Resource Centre Fugu Project (Fugu rubripes)
(*bb*) Ensembl Fugu genome browser
(*cc*) MEPD—Medaka Expression Pattern Database
(*dd*) ArkDB—Sea Bass, Salmon genome databases
(*ee*) ZFIN—Zebrafish Information Network
(*ff*) Ensembl Zebrafish genome browser

Mitochondrion and chloroplast

(*a*) GOBASE—Organelle Genome Database
(*b*) MitoDat—Mendelian Inheritance and the Mitochondrion db (mitochondrial nuclear gen
(*c*) C.caldarium—Cyanidium caldarium strain RK1 chloroplast genome

Insects

(*a*) Drosophila UniProtKB/Swiss-Prot entries, gene names and cross-references to FlyBase
(*b*) FlyBase—Drosophila genetic and molecular db

(*c*) BDGP—Berkeley Drosophila Genome Project
(*d*) FlyView—Drosophila image db
(*e*) Homophila—Human Disease to Drosophila gene db
(*f*) AnoDB—Anopheles gambiae db
(*g*) Ensembl Anopheles gambiae genome browser

Invertebrates

(*a*) WormBase—C.elegans db [Mirror at Sanger]
(*b*) C.elegans WWW server—at University of Texas Southwestern
(*c*) Ensembl C.elegans genome browser
(*d*) NEXTDB—The Nematode Expression Pattern DataBase
(*e*) C.elegans UniProtKB/Swiss-Prot entries, gene names and cross-references to

WormPep

(*a*) WormPep—C.elegans proteins db
(*b*) WorfDB—C. elegans ORFeome cloning project
(*c*) Dictyostelium discoideum UniProtKB/Swiss-Prot entries, gene names and cross

References to DictyBase

(*a*) DictyBase—Dictyostelium discoideum db
(*b*) DictyDb—Dictyostelium discoideum db
(*c*) Dictyostelium Genome Sequencing project at BCM
(*d*) Cone shells Web site
(*e*) Parasite genomes db and resources
(*f*) PlasmoDB—P.falciparum genome db
(*g*) Malaria—WHO - Malaria db (from WHO)
(*h*) P.falciparum Sanger—P.falciparum genome project at Sanger
(*i*) P.falciparum—Plasmodium falciparum Gene Sequence Tag project
(*j*) Malaria parasite metabolic pathways
(*k*) GiardiaDB
(*l*) LGN—Leishmania major Genome Project
(*m*) ToxoDB—Toxoplasma gondii genome project

(*n*) Trypanosoma brucei genome project
(*o*) Trypanosoma cruzi genome project
(*p*) kDNA—Kinetoplast Minicircle Sequence db

Plants

(1) NAL - AGIS—Access to many plant genome databases at the National Agricultural Library
(2) Mendel—Plant gene nomenclature database from CPGN
(3) FLAGdb++—Integrative database around plant genomes
(4) Arabidopsis UniProtKB/Swiss-Prot entries, gene names and WWW servers
(5) TAIR—The Arabidopsis Information Resource
(6) MATDB—MIPS Arabidopsis thaliana db
(7) AMPL—Arabidopsis Membrane Protein Library
(8) Arabidopsis at PlaCe—Site with info on P450, glucosyltransferases, etc.
(9) Gramene—A comparative mapping resource for grains
(10) Oryza sativa UniProtKB/Swiss-Prot entries, gene names and WWW servers
(11) RGP—Rice Genome Research Program
(12) Oryzabase—Japanese rice genome db
(13) Rice genome annotation project—at MSU (Michigan State University)
(14) BeanGenes—Beans genome db
(15) Brassica Genome Gateway
(16) ChlamyDB—Chlamydomonas reinhardtii genome db
(17) CoffeeDNA—Coffee genomics web site
(18) CottonDB—Cotton genome db
(19) MaizeDb—Maize genome db
(20) Pisum sativum (pea) web site (in russian)
(21) TIGR Potato—TIGR Potato Functional Genomics project (at JCVI)
(22) Snapdragon (*A.*majus) web site
(23) DragonDB—Snapdragon Database
(24) SorghumDB—Sorghum genome db
(25) DFCI GmGI—DFCI Soybean Gene Index
(26) SoyBase—Soybean genome db

(27) SoyBase metabolic db—Metabolic subset of the soybean genome db
(28) DFCI LeGI—DFCI Tomato Gene Index
(29) Dendrome—Forest trees genome db

Fungi

(*a*) Ensembl Yeast (S.cerevisiae) genome browser
(*b*) FGSC—Fungal Genetics Stock Center
(*c*) Genolevures—Genomic Exploration of the Hemiascomycete Yeasts
(*d*) FGI—Fungal genome initiative at the Broad Institute
(*e*) Fungal genome databases at MIPS
(*f*) Fungal genomes at the Sanger Institute
(*g*) FGR—Fungal Genome Resource
(*h*) MycoBank
(*i*) Yeast (S. cerevisiae) UniProtKB/Swiss-Prot entries, gene names and cross-references to SGD
(j) CYGD—MIPS Comprehensive Yeast Genome db
(*k*) SGD—Saccharomyces genome db
(*l*) Yeast snoRNA—Yeast small nucleolar RNAs db
(*m*) YTPdb—Yeast Transport Protein db
(*n*) YMPL—Yeast Membrane Protein Library
(*o*) YRC—Yeast Resource Center
(*p*) PROPHECY—Profiling of Phenotypic Characteristics in Yeast
(*q*) SCMD—Saccharomyces Cerevisiae Morphological db
(*r*) GPofYPF—Global Profiling of Yeast Protein Function
(*s*) Saccharomyces Genomes—Finding functional features in Saccharomyces Genomes by phylogenetic footprinting
(*t*) Yeast Comparative Genomics
(*u*) S.pombe UniProtKB/Swiss-Prot entries, gene names and WWW servers
(*v*) GeneDB S.Pombe-Schizosaccharomyces pombe GeneDB
(*w*) S.pombe genome project
(*x*) PombeNet—Forsburg lab pombe pages
(*y*) AGD—Ashbya genome db
(*z*) Aspergillus nidulans db

(*aa*) The Aspergillus web site

(*bb*) C. albicans UniProtKB/Swiss-Prot entries, gene names and WWW servers

(*cc*) CGD—Candida Genome db

(*dd*) C. albicans physical map—Candida albicans server at the Univ. of Minnesota

(*ee*) Candida albicans pages—Candida albicans at the NRC/BRI

(*ff*) CandidaDB—Candida albicans GenoList browser at Institut Pasteur

(*gg*) Cryptococcus neoformans Genome Project

(*hh*) FGDB—Fusarium graminearum Genome db

(*ii*) Kluyveromyces lactis annotation db

(*jj*) MNCDB—MIPS Neurospora crassa db

(*kk*) Neurospora crassa db

(*ll*) NGP—Neurospora crassa genome project at New Mexico

(*mm*) Neurospora crassa Gene List

(*nn*) MUMDB—MIPS Ustilago maydis db

(*oo*) PC—Pneumocystis carinii genome project

(*pp*) Phycomyces Web site—Resource site for scientists working on Phycomyces

Bacteria

- WDCM—World Data Center for Microorganisms
- List of Bacterial Names with Standing in Nomenclature
- List of complete bacterial proteomes in Swiss-Prot (HAMAP)
- CBS—CBS Genome Atlas Database
- CMR—TIGR Comprehensive Microbial Ressource
- GIB—Genome information broker for Microbial genomes
- GOLD Genomes On-line Database
- HOBACGEN—Homologous Bacterial Genes db
- Comparison of the transport capabilities of bacterial genomes - from Ian Paulsen
- BPGD—Bacterial polysaccharide gene db
- Bacterial quorum sensing
- MicrobeWorld—Educational site on microbes

- E.coli UniProtKB/Swiss-Prot entries, gene names and cross-references to EcoGene
- EcoWeb/EcoGene—Very comprehensive E.coli db
- ECCE—E.coli Cell Envelope Protein Data Collection
- ECDC—E.coli db collection
- EcoCyc—Encyclopaedia of E.coli genes and metabolism
- EchoBASE
- GenProtEC—E.coli genome and proteome db
- Colibri—E.coli GenoList browser at Institut Pasteur
- ECGC—E.coli Genome Center at Wisconsin University
- DDBJ E.coli—E.coli home page at DDBJ
- Regulon DB
- B.subtilis UniProtKB/Swiss-Prot entries, gene names and WWW servers
- SubtiList—Bacillus subtilis GenoList browser at Institut Pasteur
- NRSub—Bacillus subtilis non-redundant db
- DBTBS—Db of B.subtilis promoters and transcription factors
- *A*.actinomycetemcomitans—Actinobacillus actinomycetemcomitans strain HK1651 genome project
- B.stearothermophilus—Bacillus stearothermophilus strain 10 genome project
- Bordetella species genome projects at Sanger Institute—bronchiseptica strain RB50, parapertussis strain 1822 and pertussis strain Tohama I
- BbDB—Borrelia burgdorferi B31 genome db at JCVI-CMR
- Brucella abortus strain 2308 UniProtKB/Swiss-Prot entries, gene names and WWW servers
- Brucella abortus strain 9-941 UniProtKB/Swiss-Prot entries, gene names and WWW servers
- Brucella melitensis strain 16M UniProtKB/Swiss-Prot entries, gene names and WWW servers
- Brucella suis strain 1330 UniProtKB/Swiss-Prot entries, gene names and WWW servers
- B.aphidicola (subsp. Acyrthosiphon pisum) UniProtKB/Swiss-Prot entries, gene names and WWW servers
- B.aphidicola (subsp. Schizaphis graminum) UniProtKB/Swiss-Prot entries, gene names and WWW servers

- C.jejuni—Campylobacter jejuni genome project
- C.muridarum—Chlamydia muridarum strain MoPn genome db at JCVI-CMR
- C.pneumoniae AR39—Chlamydia pneumoniae strain AR39 genome db at JCVI-CMR
- C.pneumoniae J138—Chlamydia pneumoniae strain J138 genome db at JCVI-CMR
- Chromobacterium violaceum—Brazilian Genome
- C.michiganensis Claviabacter michiganensis subsp. sepdonicus genome project at Sanger Institute
- C.difficile—Clostridium difficile strain 630 genome project at Sanger Institute
- C.diphtheriae—Corynebacterium diphtheriae strain NCTC 13129 genome project at Sanger Institute
- Coxiella burnetii strain RSA 493 UniProtKB/Swiss-Prot entries, gene names and WWW servers
- CyanoBase—The Genome Database for Cyanobacteria
- CyanoList—Synechocystis PCC6803 and Anabaena PCC7120 GenoList browser at Institut Pasteur
- DrDB—Deinococcus radiodurans strain R1 genome db at JCVI-CMR
- E.ruminantium—Ehrlichia ruminantium (formerly Cowdria ruminantium) genome project at Sanger Institute
- H.influenzae UniProtKB/Swiss-Prot entries, gene names and WWW servers
- HiDB—Haemophilus influenzae genome db at JCVI-CMR
- H.pylori UniProtKB/Swiss-Prot entries, gene names and WWW servers
- HpDB—Helicobacter pylori strain 26695 genome db at JCVI-CMR
- PyloriGene—Helicobacter pylori GenoList browser at Institut Pasteur
- L.lactis—Lactobacillus lactis subsp. lactis strain IL1403 genome db
- L.plantarum—Lactobacillus plantarum genome project
- LegioList—Legionella pneumophila Paris strain and Legionella pneumophila Lens strain GenoList browser at Institut Pasteur
- ListiList—Listeria monocytogenes and Listeria innocua GenoList browser at Institut Pasteur
- BoviList—Mycobacterium bovis strain AF2122/97 GenoList browser at Institut Pasteur

- Mycobacterium—Mycobacterium genome projects at Sanger Institute
- Leproma—Mycobacterium leprae strain TN genome db
- TubercuList—Mycobacterium tuberculosis strain H37Rv GenoList browser at Institut Pasteur
- MtDB—Mycobacterium tuberculosis strain Oshkosh genome db at JCVI-CMR
- M.tuberculosis structural genomics consortium
- BuruList—Mycobacterium ulcerans strain Agy99 GenoList browser at Institut Pasteur
- M.genitalium UniProtKB/Swiss-Prot entries, gene names and WWW servers
- MgDB—Mycoplasma genitalium genome db at JCVI-CMR
- M.pneumoniae UniProtKB/Swiss-Prot entries, gene names and WWW servers
- M.pneumoniae—Mycoplasma pneumoniae genome project
- MypuList—Mycoplasma pulmonis GenoList browser at Institut Pasteur
- Mycoplasma synoviae genome db—Brazilian Genome
- Nesseria—Neisseria genome projects at Sanger Institute
- N.meningitidis B—Neisseria meningitidis serogroup B strain MC58 genome db at JCVI-CMR
- N.europaea—Nitrosomonas europaea genome project
- PhotoList—Photorhabdus luminescens strain TT01 GenoList browser at Institut Pasteur
- P.marinus—Prochlorococcus marinus genome project
- P.aeruginosa project—Pseudomonas aeruginosa genome project
- R.solanacearum—Ralstonia solanacearum genome project
- Rhizobium pNGR234a UniProtKB/Swiss-Prot entries, gene names and WWW servers
- RhizoBase—The Genome Database for Rhizobia
- Rhizobium pNGR234a analysis
- Rhodobacter sphaeroides genome db
- R.palustris—Rhodopseudomonas palustris genome project
- RicBase—Rickettsia conorii strain Malish 7 genome project
- R.bellii strain RML369-C UniProtKB/Swiss-Prot entries, gene names and WWW servers

- R.conorii strain Malish 7 UniProtKB/Swiss-Prot entries, gene names and WWW servers
- R.felis strain URRWXCa12 UniProtKB/Swiss-Prot entries, gene names and WWW servers
- R.prowazekii UniProtKB/Swiss-Prot entries, gene names and WWW servers
- R.typhi strain Wilmington UniProtKB/Swiss-Prot entries, gene names and WWW servers
- Salmonella – Salmonella genome projects at Sanger Institute
- S.meliloti – Sinorhizobium meliloti genome project
- AureoList – Staphylococcus aureus strains N315 and Mu50 GenoList browser at Institut Pasteur
- S.aureus – Staphylococcus aureus strain NCTC 8325 genome project
- SagaList – Streptococcus agalactiae strain NEM316 GenoList browser at Institut Pasteur
- StreptoPneumoList – Streptococcus pneumoniae strains R6 and Tigr4 GenoList browser at Institut Pasteur
- S.mutans – Streptococcus mutans strain UAB159 genome project
- S.pyogenes M1 – Streptococcus pyogenes strain SF370 serotype M1 genome project
- S.pyogenes – Streptococcus pyogenes genome project at Sanger Institute
- S.suis – Streptococcus suis genome project at Sanger Institute
- S.uberis – Streptococcus uberis genome project at Sanger Institute
- S.coelicolor – Streptomyces coelicolor genome project at Sanger Institute
- S.avermitilis – Streptomyces avermitilis strain MA-4680 genome project
- Synechocystis strain PCC 6803 UniProtKB/Swiss-Prot entries, gene names and WWW servers
- TmDB – Thermotoga maritima genome db at JCVI-CMR
- TpDB – Treponema pallidum genome db at JCVI-CMR
- T.whipplei – Tropheryma whipplei genome project at Sanger Institute
- U.urealyticum – Ureaplasma urealyticum genome WWW site
- VcDB – Vibrio cholerae genome db at JCVI-CMR
- X.fastidiosa – Xylella fastidiosa genome project
- Yersinia – Yersinia genome projects at Sanger Institute

Archaea

- List of complete archaeal proteomes in Swiss-Prot (HAMAP)
- UCSC Archeal Genome Browser
- *A*.pernix—Aeropyrum pernix K1 genome db
- AfDB—Archaeoglobus fulgidus genome db at JCVI-CMR
- Halobacterium NRC-1—Halobacterium strain NRC-1 genome project
- M.jannaschii UniProtKB/Swiss-Prot entries, gene names and WWW servers
- MjDB—Methanococcus jannaschii genome db at JCVI-CMR
- Pyrococcus abyssi genome and re-annotation db
- Pyrococcus sp. OT3
- Sulfolobus solfataricus P2 genome project
- T.volcanium—Thermoplasma volcanium genome project

Viruses and phages

(*a*) All the virology on the WWW—links to virology WWW servers by David M. Sander

(*b*) ICTVdB—Universal virus taxonomy db

(*c*) ViralZone—Portal to viral UniProtKB/Swiss-Prot entries

(*d*) Adenoviruses web site

(*e*) HCVDB—Hepatitis C virus db

(*f*) HIV—HIV and related species db

(*g*) HPV—Human papillomaviruses db

(*h*) Picornavirus—Picornavirus home page and access to db

(*i*) VirOligo—virus-specific oligonucleotides database

(*j*) PhageBase

(*k*) Phage Sequence Databank at Sdsu Center for Universal Microbial Sequencing (currently not working)

(*l*) The Bacteriophage Ecology Group

(*m*) GOLD—Genomes On-line db

(*n*) DOGS—Database of genome sizes

Human mutation databases/resources

- HGMD—Human Gene Mutation db
- SVD—EBI Sequence variation db

- HGVbase
- HGVS—The Human Genome Variation Society
- LOVD—Leiden Open Variation database
- The International HapMap Project
- dbSNP—Human single nucleotide polymorphism (SNP) db
- ALFRED—Allele Frequency Db
- SeattleSNPs—UW-FHCRC Variation Discovery Resource
- PicSNP—Catalog of non-synonymous SNP
- List of mutation databases from OMIM
- List of mutation databases from IMT (Finland)
- ADAbase—Human adenosine deaminase (ADA) mutation db
- Albinism Database
- Albumin Web site
- AR mutations—Human androgen receptor mutation db
- Antithrombin mutation db
- BIOMDB—Db of mutations causing tetrahydrobiopterin deficiencies
- BLMbase—Human BLM mutation db (Bloom syndrome)
- BTKbase—Human BTK mutation db (X-linked agammaglobulinemia)
- CC_dbMD The Congenital Cataract Mutation Database
- CD3Ebase—Human CD3E mutation db
- CD3Gbase—Human CD3G mutation db
- CD40Lbase—Human CD40 ligand mutation db
- CD40Lbase—Human CD40 ligand mutation db
- COL1/3 mutation—Human Type I and III collagen mutation db
- Connexin-deafness—Human connexins mutation db
- CFTR mutation—Human cystic fibrosis mutation db (CFTR)
- KMbloodDB—Blood disease genes db
- KMbrainDB—Brain disease genes db
- KMcancerDB—Cancer disease genes db
- KMearDB—Ear disease genes db
- KMeyeDB—Eye disease genes db
- KMheartDB—Heart disease genes db
- KMmuscleDB—Muscle disease genes db

- KMsyndromeDB
- MaiDB (autoimmune)
- G6PD—Human G6PD deficiency resource
- G6PDdb—Human G6PD mutation db
- GNAS1—Human GNAS1 mutation db
- HAMSTeRS—The Haemophilia A Mutation db and Factor VII Resource site
- Haemophilia B mutation db- Factor IX
- HbVar—Hemoglobin variants db
- Hereditary hearing loss homepage
- LDLR mutation—Human LDLR mutation db (Familial hypercholesterolemia)
- NCF1base—Human NCF1 mutation db
- NCF2base—Human NCF2 mutation db
- Neuromuscular diseases web site
- NCL—Neuronal Ceroid Lipofuscinoses mutation db
- OCRL1—OCRL1 mutation db (Lowe Syndrome)
- Cytochrome P450 alleles nomenclature
- IARC TP53 mutation db—International Agency for Research on Cancer
- Germline p53 mutation db—University of Prague db of germline p53 mutations
- PAHdb—Human phenylalanine hydroxylase (PAH) mutation db
- Prion—Wikipedia Prion and prion disease
- RAG1base—Human RAG1 mutation db
- RAG2base—Human RAG2 mutation db
- RB1base—Human retinoblastoma-associated protein (RB) mutation db
- RetNet—Retinal Information Network
- Retina International Scientific Newsletter—Information on Retinal genes, proteins and diseases
- Alsod.org—ALS/SOD1 genetic mutations db
- TGDB—Tumor gene db
- VMD2 mutation—Human VMD2 mutation db
- vWF mutation—Human von Willebrand factor (vWF) mutation db

- WRN—Human WRN mutation db (Warner disease)
- X-ALD mutation—Human ABCD1 mutation db

Gene(s)/protein(s) specific databases/resources

- Human ABC transporters
- ABCISSE—ABC systems : Information on Sequence Structure and Evolution
- ADAMTS—Apte lab ADAMTS and ADAMTSL resource
- Human albumin Web site
- Nomenclature and entries of allergens in UniProtKB/Swiss-Prot
- Allergen sequence db
- Allergome—A platform for allergen knowledge
- SDAP—Structural database of allergenic proteins
- Alginate genes—Pseudomomonas alginate production genes
- Entries of aminoacyl-tRNA synthetases in UniProtKB/Swiss-Prot
- AARSDB—Aminoacyl-tRNA synthetases db
- Androgen Receptor Gene Mutations Database
- AMSDb—Antimicrobial sequences db
- Antibody resource page—Links to antibody related Web resources
- Linscott's Directory of Immunological and Biological Reagents
- AraC-XylS—A db on a family of helix-turn-helix transcription factors from
- bacteria
- Bcl-2 family database
- Blood group antigens in UniProtKB/Swiss-Prot
- BRENDA—Db of enzyme functional data
- EF-hand CaBP—EF-hand calcium-binding proteins data library
- CAZy—Carbohydrate-Active enZYmes Web site
- CBS domain—Cystathionine Beta Synthase domain
- CD antigens entries and nomenclature in UniProtKB/Swiss-Prot
- cpnDB—A Chaperonin Database
- CSDBase—Cold shock domain db
- COPE—Cytokines On-line Pathfinder Encyclopaedia
- dbCFC—Cytokine family db

- DPInteract—DNA-Proteins interactions db
- EMP—Enzymes and Metabolic Pathways db
- ENZYME—Enzymes nomenclature db
- Worthington enzyme manual
- EpoDB—Erythropoiesis gene expression db (Epo GED)
- ESTHER—Esterases and alpha/beta hydrolase enzymes
- Estrogen Receptor Resource
- Expansins web site
- Modules—Extracellular proteins modules (domains)
- FADPNR—FAD-dependent pyridine nucleotide oxidoreductases
- Flavodoxins
- FYVE finger domain
- Globin—Globin gene server
- Glucocorticoid Receptor Resource
- Nomenclature and entries of Glycosyl hydrolases in UniProtKB/Swiss-Prot
- 7TM—Entries of 7-transmembrane G-linked receptors in UniProtKB/Swiss-Prot
- GPCRDB—G protein-coupled receptor db (7TM) at EMBL
- GPCRs database
- GRR—Glucocorticoid receptor resource
- SSFA-GPHR—Glycoprotein Hormone Receptors database
- Arabidopsis Glycosyltransferases Family 1
- GnRH—Gonadotropin-releasing hormones (GnRH) family
- Histone—Histones db
- HIVdb—HIV protease db
- HORDE—Human Olfactory Receptor Data Exploratorium
- Hox proteins—Nomenclature and entries of vertebrate homeotic Hox proteins in UniProtKB/Swiss-Prot
- IMGT—ImMunoGeneTics db [Mirror at EBI]
- InBase—Inteins db from the New England Biolabs
- Integrins—from Wikipedia
- Initiation factors—Entries of translation initiation factors in UniProtKB/Swiss-Prot

- LGIC—Ligand Gated Ion Channel subunit db
- Voltage-gated Ion Channels
- KEGG—Kyoto Encyclopedia of Genes and Genomes
- Klotho—Biochemical compounds declarative db
- LED—Lipase Engineering Database
- MDB—Metalloprotein Site Database and Browser
- EPIMHC—A curated database of MHC ligands
- Mitochondrial carriers pages from Nelson's lab
- NPD—Nuclear Protein db
- NucleaRDB—Federated db on nuclear receptors
- P450—Directory of P450-containing systems
- Arabidopsis P450 Web site
- IARC p53 db—IARC db of somatic p53 mutations
- PDE—Phosphodiesterases
- Peroxibase—the Peroxidase database
- Classification and entries of peptidases in UniProtKB/Swiss-Prot
- MEROPS—Peptidase db
- PLACE—Plant cis-acting regulatory DNA elements db
- KinBase
- PKR—Protein Kinase Resource
- PatBase—P-type ATPase db
- PPAR—Peroxisome Proliferator-Activated Receptor resource
- Reactome—a curated knowledgebase of biological pathways
- REBASE—Restriction enzymes and methylases db
- Classification and entries of restriction enzymes/methylases in UniProtKB/Swiss-Prot
- Familes and entries of ribosomal proteins in UniProtKB/Swiss-Prot
- RNA Helicase database
- RNase P—Ribonuclease P db
- SABIO Reaction Kinetics Database
- SPAD—Signaling pathway db
- SRPDB—Signal Recognition Particle db
- SNF2—SNF2 family protein resource
- TTD—Therapeutic Targets Database

- TRANSFAC—Transcription factors db
- TFII—Basal transcription factors
- TRANSPATH—Signal Transduction Browser
- TC-DB—Transport Classification System from Milton Saier
- VDR—Vitamin D Nuclear Receptor
- WD-repeat—WD-repeat proteins family
- Wnt homepage
- WormPep—C.elegans proteins db
- YTPdb—Yeast Transport Protein db
- Tox-Prot—The UniProtKB/Swiss-Prot Toxin Annotation Program
- ConoServer
- The Venom Composition—Information on conotoxins from a Web site on cone shells
- International venom and toxin db
- Snake database at Natural Toxins Research Center

Post-translational modifications databases and resources

(*a*) DSDBASE—Disulfide database (derived from 3D data)
(*b*) GlycoSuiteDB—Db of glycan structures
(*c*) LIPID MAPS—LIPID Metabolites And Pathways Strategy
(*d*) GlycateBase—Database of glycation data for epsilon amino groups of lysines
(*e*) O-GlycBase—O-glycosylated proteins db
(*f*) Phospho.ELM—Phosphorylation sites db
(*g*) PhosphoSite—Db of phosphorylation sites in human and mouse proteomes
(*h*) DOLOP Db of bacterial lipoproteins
(*i*) UbiProt—Db of ubiquitylated proteins
(*j*) RESID—Db of Amino Acid Modifications
(*k*) Delta Mass—Db of mass of Post-Translational Modifications

Phylogenetics and taxonomy databases and resources

(*a*) COG and KOG—Phylogenetic classification of proteins encoded in complete genomes
(*b*) eggNog—Automated construction and annotation of orthologous groups of genes

(*c*) EGO—Eukaryotic Gene Orthologs
(*d*) Ensembl Compara—Genome-wide species comparisons
(*e*) HOGENOM—Homologous Sequences in Complete Genomes Database
(*f*) HOVERGEN—Homologous Vetebrate Genes Database
(*g*) InParanoid—Eukaryotic ortholog groups
(*h*) KO—KEGG Orthology:
(*i*) Metazome—Phylogenomic analysis of metazoan gene families
(*j*) Optic—Orthologous and paralogous transcripts in clades
(*k*) OMA—Orthologs Matrix Project (OMA)
(*l*) OrthoDB Hierarchical catalog of eukaryotic orthologs
(*m*) OrthoMCL DB Ortholog grouping for protein sequences from multiple genomes
(*n*) PhylomeDB—Database for phylomes (collections of phylogenetic trees for all proteins encoded in a given genome)
(*o*) P-POD—Princeton Protein Orthology Database with an emphasis on providing information about disease-related genes
(*p*) Protein Clusters—NCBI collection of related protein sequences (clusters)
(*q*) PhyloFacts—Pre-calculated structural and phylogenomic analyses of protein families and domains
(*r*) TreeFam—Tree families database of phylogenetic trees of animal genes
(*s*) CluSTr—Automatic classification of UniProtKB proteins into groups of related proteins
(*t*) HomoloGene—Automated detection of homologs among the annotated genes of several completely sequenced eukaryotic genomes
(*u*) ProtoNet—Classification of the proteins into hierarchical clusters
(*v*) NCBI Taxonomy Browser
(*w*) Taxonomy—UniProt Taxonomy Browser
(*x*) The Tree of life—Collection of WWW pages on phylogeny and biodiversity of organisms
(*y*) TreeBASE—Relational db of phylogenetic information

Gene expression databases and resources

(*a*) 4DXpress—a database for cross-species expression pattern comparisons
(*b*) ArrayExpress—MicroArray informatics at the EBI

(*c*) Bgee—Retrieve and compare gene expression patterns across species
(*d*) BioGPS—The Gene Portal Hub
(*e*) CleanEx—database of gene expression profiles
(*f*) ExpressDB—Yeast and E.coli RNA expression db
(*g*) GeneX—An open source Gene Expression database
(*h*) GEO—Gene Expression Omnibus
(*i*) GXD—MGI Gene Expression Database (mouse)
(*j*) RAD—RNA abundance db
(*k*) SMD—Stanford microarray db
(*l*) MILANO—Microarray Literature-based Annotation
(*m*) Genevestigator—a multi-organism, novel type of online meta-analysis tool for gene expression
(*n*) GEMLeR—Gene Expression Machine Learning Repository

Patents databases

(*a*) DPD—DNA Patent db
(*b*) USDA Agricultural Biotechnology Intellectual Property
(*c*) Esp@cenet—Patent information database from the European Patent Office (worldwide coverage)
(*d*) FindThatPatent
(*e*) FreePatentsOnline—access to millions of patents
(*f*) WikiPatents—the largest database of patents open for public comment on the internet
(*g*) Germany Patent database—with full-text and one-click patent search
(*h*) Japanese Patents and Inventions
(*i*) USPTO patent db—USA Patent and Trademark Office patent db

References (bibliographic databases)

(*a*) PubMed Medline server
(*b*) BioMedSearch—an enhanced version of the NIH PubMed/MedLine search
(*c*) AGRICOLA—AGRICultural OnLine Access; ref. db from NAL
(*d*) RefDoc (ex-Article@INIST)—Scientific and Technical Information Institute articles and monographs db
(*e*) SeqAnalRef—Sequence analysis bibliographic references

Dictionaries, protocols, courses, nomenclature, etc.

- Biology Reference
- BioTech's life science dictionary
- DCB—Dictionary of cell biology by Julian Dow
- DNA Microbiology Guide Online
- AAnP—IUPAC-IUBMB nomenclature for amino acids and peptides
- Amino acids 2—Another information page on amino acids (from Berlin Free Univ.)
- Carbohydrates—IUPAC-IUBMB nomenclature for carbohydrates
- Codon Usage db
- Glossary of Biochemistry and Molecular Biology—by David M. Glick
- Primer on molecular genetics—from the US Department of Energy
- Ion Source—Mass spectrometry resource
- Sequence similarity searches primer—from Keith Robison/Harvard
- Pedestrian guide to analysing sequence databases—from Burkhard Rost and Reinard Schneider
- Quick Guides—EMBnet Quick guides
- BioActivity—Protein sequence and structure analysis: a practical guide
- Protein Structures Guide
- VSNS BioComputing courses
- Cold Spring Harbor Protocols
- Abbreviations of chemical compounds
- UniProtKB/Swiss-Prot list of nomenclature related references for proteins
- GO—Gene Ontology Consortium WWW site
- HUGO nomenclature committee
- JCBN—IUPAC-IUB Joint commission on Biochemical Nomenclature (JCBN)
- Nobel Foundation Website
- The Nobel prize Internet Archive
- UniProt Taxonomy Browser
- NCBI Taxonomy
- LPSN—List of Prokaryotic Names with Standing in Nomenclature
- ISIS—International Species Information System

- Species 2000—Project to provide in an electronic form the names and taxonomy of all known species

Biological software and databases catalog servers

- CLC Free Workbench—A desktop program including a number of algorithms for DNA, RNA, and protein analyses. Available for Linux, MacOS X and Windows
- CLC Protein Workbench—A desktop program including a number of advanced algorithms for protein sequence analysis. Available for Linux, MacOS X and Windows
- CodonCode Aligner—Sequence assembly and alignment
- LabLife—Lab tools for your lab research
- BioCatalogue
- ChemSynthesis—Chemical Database
- LIC Generator—A web-based software for Ligation Independent Cloning vector and primer design
- Genamix Software Seek

Gateways (portals) to Life Science resources

- Antibody Directory—A comprehensive portal for antibodies with a broad collection of research antibodies available world over
- Biofind—Biotechnology industry information, gossip and news
- Bioinformatik.de—Web directory for bioinformatics
- BioNetbook—Institut Pasteur gateway to biosites
- Bioplanet—The bioinformatics homepage
- BIOPPS—Science and Technology Biocluster de Mexico
- Bioexplorer.net
- Biotaq.com
- BioTech
- drugdevelopment-technology.com
- Enzyme Directory—An exclusive portal for Enzymes, Substrates, Inhibitors and Recombinant proteins.

Some biological societies and organizations

- APS—American Peptide Society
- ASCB—The American Society for Cell Biology

- ASHG—American Society of Human Genetics
- ATC-LGCC—American Type Culture Collection
- Biochemical Society
- BSA—Botanical Society of America
- CSBMCB—Canadian Society of Biochemistry and Molecular and Cell Biology
- EFBF—European Federation of Biophysics
- EGF—European Genetics Foundation
- EMBO—European Molecular Biology Organization
- ESEB—European Society for Evolutionary Biology
- ESHG—European Society of Human Genetics
- FAOBMB—Federation of Asian and Oceanian Biochemists and Molecular Biologists
- FASEB—Federation of American Societies for Experimental Biology
- FEBS—Federation of European Biochemistry Societies
- HUGO—HUman Genome Organization
- HUPO—HUman Proteome Organization
- IUBMB—International Union of Biochemistry and Molecular Biology
- IUPAC—International Union of Pure and Applied Chemistry
- MSA—Mycological Society of America
- PPI—Plasma Proteome Institute
- PRF—Protein Research Foundation
- SDB—Society for Developmental Biology
- SGM—Society for General Microbiology
- SICB—Society for Integrative and Comparative Biology
- DOI—Digital Object Identifier foundation
- BioJava Project—International association of developers of Java tools for bioinformatics
- Bioperl Project—International association of developers of Perl tools for bioinformatics
- Biopython Project—International association of developers of Python tools for bioinformatics
- ISCB—International Society for Computational Biology
- OMG LSR—Object Management Group Life Science Research task force

BIOCOMPUTING SERVERS HOMEPAGES

Europe

- EBI—European Bioinformatics Institute
- EMBnet—European Molecular Biology Network
- EMBL—EMBL Biocomputing unit
- SIB—Swiss Institute of Bioinformatics
- EMBnet CH—Switzerland EMBnet node
- ISREC—ISREC/SIB Computational Cancer Genomics group (Lausanne/Swizerland)
- CBRG—Computational Biochemistry Research Group (Zurich/Switzerland)
- ABIM—Atelier BioInformatique (Marseille/FR)
- B3E—Bioinformatique/Biostatistique/Biomathematique/Epidemiologie (Paris/FR)
- Genethon—Genethon (Evry/FR)
- GeneStream—Institut de Génétique Humaine (Montpellier/FR)
- GENOSCOPE—Centre National de Séquencage (Evry/FR)
- GenoStar—Consortium for the development of a bioinformatic platform
- IGS—Information Génétique et Structurale (Structural and Genetic Information Laboratory) (Marseille/FR)
- IMPBIO—Informatique, Mathématiques, Physique en Biologie moléculaire
- Pasteur—Institut Pasteur (Paris/FR)
- PBIL—Pole Bio-informatique Lyonnais (Lyon/FR)
- Sanger—Sanger Centre (Hinxton/U.K.)
- BMM—Biomolecular Modelling laboratory at ICRF (London/U.K.)
- BSM—Biomolecular Structure and Modelling group at UCL (London/U.K.)
- Manchester—Manchester University Bioinformatics unit (U.K.)
- HUSAR—Biocomputing Service at DKFZ
- AG BIODV—Software Development for Molecular Biology at Helmholtz Zentrum (Germany)
- FLI—Genome Analysis in Complex Diseases, Ageing and Model Organisms (Germany)

- MDC:Bioinf—Department of Bionformatic of the Max Delbruck Center for Molecular Medicine (Germany)
- MIPS—Munich Information Centre for Protein Sequences (Germany)
- PZR—Bioinformatics at the Proteome Center Rostock (Germany)
- BEN—Belgium EMBnet node
- CBS—Center for Biological Sequence Analysis (Technical University of Denmark)
- CSC BioBox—Resources for Bioscientists
- ABC—Agricultural Biotechnology Center (Budapest/Hungary)
- Telethon Italy
- CMBI—Center for Molecular and Biomolecular Bioinformatics; Netherland EMBnet node
- BIO—Biotechnology Centre of Oslo; Norway EMBnet node
- IBB—Institute of Biochemistry and Biophysics (Warsaw); Poland EMBnet node
- IGC—Bioinformatics and Computational Unit of the Instituto Gulbenkian de Ciencia; Portugal EMBnet Node
- Belozersky Institute—GeneBee Molecular Biology server (Moscow); Russia EMBnet node
- MGS—Molecular Biological Server (Novosibirsk/Russia)
- CNB—Centro Nacional de Biotecnologia; Spain EMBnet node
- BMC—BioMedical Centre at Uppsala; Sweden EMBnet node
- KISAC—Karolinska Institute (KI) Sequence Analysis Computer
- LCB—Linnaeus Centre for Bioinformatics
- SBC—Stockholm Bioinformatics Center

USA and Canada

- NCBI—National Center for Biotechnology Information
- ABCC—Advanced Biomedical Computing Center at the NCI
- ACGT—Advanced Center for Genome Technology at the University of Oklahoma
- BCM HGC—Baylor College of Medicine Human Genome Center
- BDGP—Berkeley Drosophila Genome Project
- BioTech—Life Sciences Resources and Reference Tools

- Biotechnology—National Agricultural Library - Biotechnology
- BMERC—Biomolecular Engineering Research Center
- BROAD Institute
- CBIL—Computational Biology and Informatics Laboratory at the University of Pennsylvania
- CCB—Washington University Center for Computational Biology
- CUBIC—Columbia University Bioinformatics Center/RostLab
- JCVI—J. Craig Venter Institute
- JGI—Doe Joint Genome Institute
- NCGR—National Center for Genome Resources
- NIH—Computational Molecular Biology at NIH
- UCLA—UCLA Bioinformatics Institute
- Bioinformatics & Research Computing at Whitehead Institute
- CCB—Centre for Computational Biology at the Hospital for sick children

Asia

- APBioNet—Asia-Pacific Bioinformatics network
- BIDD—Bioinformatics and Drug Design group (National University/ Singapore)
- DIC—Bioinformatics Centre at the University of Pune
- Japanese GenomeNet
- NIG—National Institute of Genetics of Japan
- KDRI—Kazusa DNA Research Institute
- CBI—Peking Center of Bioinformatics; Chinese EMBnet node
- MICRO-NET—Microbial Information Network of China
- HKBIC—Hong Kong Bioinformatics Center
- BRIC—Biological Research Information Center (Korea)
- MGRC—Malaysian Genomics Resource Centre
- BIC—BioInformatics Center of the National University of Singapore

Australia

- APBioNet—Asia-Pacific Bioinformatics network
- ANGIS—Australian National Genomic Information Service
- ANU—Australian National University Genomic Interactions group
- APAF—Australian Proteome Analysis Facility

Others

- HUJI—Hebrew University of Jerusalem genomic and bioinformatics server
- Weizmann Bioinfo/BCU—Weizmann Institute of Science Bioinformatics and
- Biological Computing
- SANBI—South African BioInformatics Institute
- ICGEB—International Center for Genetic Engineering and Biotechnology (Trieste/Italy)
- Biotechnology and pharmaceutical companies
- Pharmaceutical Research and Manufacturers of America membership list
- Bioportfolio—Gateways to biobusiness
- 1st BASE Singapore
- 5 Prime, Inc.
- Abcam—Supplier of antibodies, kits and reagents
- Actelion
- Addgene
- Affymetrix, Inc.
- Airmid Pharmaceuticals—privately held pharmaceutical company based in
- California
- ALEXIS Biochemicals—Now Enzo Life Sciences
- Amgen
- Amplicon Express
- AMSBIO—Innovative products for genomics, proteomics and immunology
- Antibodies online
- Aptuit
- ARCA biopharma
- ARIAD Pharmaceuticals, Inc.
- AstraZeneca Pharmaceuticals
- Atheris Laboratories
- Aurora Fine Chemicals Ltd
- Basilea

- Bayer
- BD Biosciences—Becton, Dickinson and Co
- Beckman Coulter Genomics
- Bend Research Inc.—Innovators in Pharmaceutical and Health Science Technologies
- Biacore Life Sciences
- Bio Balance, Inc.
- Bio-Synthesis Inc
- Biogen Idec
- BioLaboratorio
- BioPur AG—Proteins - Enzymes - Reagents
- Bio-Rad Laboratories, Inc.
- Biosci Register—The Online Biotech Buyer's Guide
- BioSupplyUK
- BioSystematica—Gel Imagers & Gel Analysis
- BioTools
- Biotrofix
- BioVisioN GmbH
- BTC—BioSpecifics Technology Corp.
- Caprion Proteomics, Inc.
- Carbosynth—offering 2500 carbohydrates and nucleosides
- Celera
- Celldex Therapeutics—antibody-based combination immunotherapy company
- Cellectis SA—Genome Engineering
- CST—Cell Signalling Technology
- CellZome
- Centocor Ortho Biotech, Inc.
- ChanTest—The ion channel expert
- Clinical Data, Inc.
- CLL Pharma
- Clontech Laboratories, Inc.
- Cooper Pharma Ltd
- CSL Ltd

- Cytos Biotechnology
- DATAbiotech
- deCODE Genetics, Inc.
- Destiny Pharma Ltd.
- Digilab
- DNAVision
- Do-Coop Technologies Ltd
- Drug Development Technology
- easyDNA – DNA testing company
- Eli Lilly
- Emerald Biosystems – products for crystallography
- Encysive Pharmaceuticals
- Entelechon GmbH
- Entelos, Inc. – predictive biosimulation
- EnviroLogix, Inc. – Test Kits
- Enzon Pharmaceuticals, Inc.
- EraGen Biosciences – molecular assays for early detection of diseases
- Evolva Holding SA – Developing Drugs with Genetic Chemistry
- EVOTEC AG
- Esbatech – Antibody fragment therapeutics
- Exelixis Inc.
- Exclusive Chemistry – design and synthesis of organic compounds
- Fermentas
- Fine Chemicals – Fine chemicals at Spectrum Chemicals.
- G Biosciences – Proteomic products
- Gelcompany
- GENEART – DNA engineering and processing
- Genencor International, Inc.
- Genentech, Inc.
- GeneON
- Genetics Institute
- GE Healthcare
- Genfit – early prevention and treatment of cardiometabolic and neurodegenerative diseases

- Genlantis—biological reagents and protein expression tools
- Genome Express, SA
- GenScript (DNA Synthesis)—Gene/DNA Synthesis Supplier
- GenWay Biotech, Inc.
- Genzyme Co.
- Geron Co.
- GL Biochem (Shangai) Ltd
- Global Scientific—The Laboratory Supply Company
- GSK—GlaxoSmithKline
- Helix Biopharma Corp.
- HGS—Human Genome Sciences, Inc.
- Hybrigenics SA
- HyTest—Cardiac markers, disease reagents, hormones and toxins, human proteins, neuroscience products.
- Illumina, Inc.
- Incyte Pharmaceuticals, Inc.
- Integrated Genomics, Inc.
- ISCO—International Stem Cell Corporation
- International Biosciences
- Invitrogen
- Johnson & Johnson
- Jova Solutions
- Keratech Diagnostics
- KuDOS Pharmaceuticals Ltd
- LAROVA GmbH
- Lee BioSolutions, Inc.
- Ligand Pharmaceuticals, Inc
- Merck Serono
- Migenix
- Mitsui Chemicals America, Inc.
- Millennium Pharmaceuticals, Inc.
- Millipore Co.
- Miltenyi
- MOLOGEN AG

- MP Biomedicals—(formerly ICN Biomedicals & Qbiogene)
- MP Sciences
- Myriad Genetics, Inc.
- NEB—New England Biolabs, Inc.
- NGI—National Genetics Institute
- Non-linear Dynamics Ltd
- Novartis
- Novo Nordisk
- Novozymes
- Ocimum Biosolutions—BioIT, Microarrays and contract research services
- Open Biosystems—part of Thermo Fisher Scientific
- Opsona Therapeutics—drug development company specialising in the human immune system
- Organic Chemistry Portal
- P212121—Crystallography supplies, tools and chemicals
- Pfizer, Inc.
- Pharsight Corp.
- PrimerDesign
- Prionics AG
- Promega Corp.
- Protein Biotechnologies Inc.
- Proteome Factory (German version)
- Proteus Biosciences Inc.
- Protoxin Life Sciences—Genomic DNA Extraction Kit
- Prozomix—Recombinant enzymes and proteins
- ProZyme, Inc.
- QIAGEN GmbH
- Quantum Pharmaceuticals—Drug Discovery and Computational Chemistry Software
- R&D Chemicals—Rare Chemicals Database
- Randox Life Sciences
- Repligen Corp.
- Roche Bioscience

- sanofi-aventis
- SARomics Biostructures
- Scientz—manufacturer of life science instruments
- Sequenom Industrial Genomics
- Shire Pharmaceuticals Group plc
- Sigma-Aldrich
- Sirius Analytical - automated pKa, logP/D and solubility measurement
- SKS Science
- Southern Lights Biomaterials
- Simplexity Health—was Cell Tech
- SpheriTech—consultancy and production of custom synthesis of peptides, related molecules and small organics
- Syngenta
- The Genetics Company
- Thermo Scientific
- Toplab GmbH
- Transition Therapeutics Inc.
- Tyrian Diagnostics—ex-Proteome Systems Ltd
- Vernenium
- Vertex Pharmaceuticals
- WITA—Wittmann Institute of Technology and Analysis of Biomolecules GmbH
- Wyeth Pharmaceuticals—Health Care Professional Resources
- Worthington Biochemical Corp.
- Xenometrix AG
- Xerion Pharmaceuticals GmbH

REFERENCES

1. Ash LR, Orihel TC: *Atlas of Human Parasitology,* 4/e, Chicago, ASCP, 1997. *ASM News,* American Society for Microbiology, 1997, pp 590–592.
2. Baron S: *Medical Microbiology,* 4/e, New York, Churchill Livingstone, 1996.
3. Davis BD, *et al*: *Microbiology,* 4/e, New York, Harper & Row, 1990.
4. Howard BJ, Keiser JF, Smith TF, Weissfeld AS, Tilton RC: *Clinical and Pathogenic Microbiology,* 2/e, St. Louis, Mosby, 1993.
5. Levinson W, Jawetz E: *Medical Microbiology & Immunology,* 6/e, New York, McGraw-Hill, 2000.

6. Mandell GL, Douglas RG, Bennett JE: *Principles and Practice of Infectious Disease,* 3/e, New York, Wiley, 1990. *MMWR* 37:737–738, 1988. *MMWR* 38:4–7, 1989.
7. Murray PR, *et al: Manual of Clinical Microbiology,* 7/e, ASM Press, 1999.
8. Raoult D, Tilton RC: *Dictionary of Infectious Diseases,* Elsevier, New York, 2000.
9. Ryan KT (ed): *Sherris's Medical Microbiology,* 3/e, Appleton & Lange, Stamford, CT, 1994.
10. Tilton RC, Balows A, Hohnadel DC, Reiss RF: *Clinical Laboratory Medicine,* St. Louis, Mosby, 1992.
11. *Medfools Bacteriology a la chart for the USMLE I*
12. *Tortora general microbiology (2004)*
13. *Richards titon pretestmicrobiology 10th edition*
14. Lansing M Prescott, Microbiology, 5/e
15. rakesh patel, Practical microbiology 3 edition
16. pleczar, general microbiology 1st edition

Index